**DATE DUE
REMINDER**

Nov 19 '01		

WORLD
HISTORY SERIES ■ ■ ■

The Persian Empire

Titles in the World History Series

The Persian Empire

by
Don Nardo

Lucent Books, P.O. Box 289011, San Diego, CA 92198-9011

Library of Congress Cataloging-in-Publication Data

Nardo, Don, 1947–
     The Persian Empire / by Don Nardo.
          p. cm. — (World history series)
     Includes bibliographical references (p.   ) and index.
     Summary: An account of the rise and fall of the Persian
Empire, based in part on archaeological findings of the twenti-
eth century.
     ISBN 1-56006-320-3 (alk. paper)
     1. Iran—History—To 640—Juvenile literature. [1. Iran—
History—To 640.] I. Title. II. Series.
DS281.N37   1998
935—dc21   97-3081
                                                                        CIP
                                                                        AC

Contents

Foreword

Each year on the first day of school, nearly every history teacher faces the task of explaining why his or her students should study history. One logical answer to this question is that exploring what happened in our past explains how the things we often take for granted—our customs, ideas, and institutions—came to be. As statesman and historian Winston Churchill put it, "Every nation or group of nations has its own tale to tell. Knowledge of the trials and struggles is necessary to all who would comprehend the problems, perils, challenges, and opportunities which confront us today." Thus, a study of history puts modern ideas and institutions in perspective. For example, though the founders of the United States were talented and creative thinkers, they clearly did not invent the concept of democracy. Instead, they adapted some democratic ideas that had originated in ancient Greece and with which the Romans, the British, and others had experimented. An exploration of these cultures, then, reveals their very real connection to us through institutions that continue to shape our daily lives.

Another reason often given for studying history is the idea that lessons exist in the past from which contemporary societies can benefit and learn. This idea, although controversial, has always been an intriguing one for historians. Those that agree that society can benefit from the past often quote philosopher George Santayana's famous statement, "Those who cannot remember the past are condemned to repeat it." Historians who ascribe to Santayana's philosophy believe that, for example, studying the events that led up to the major world wars or other significant historical events would allow society to chart a different and more favorable course in the future.

Just as difficult as convincing students to realize the importance of studying history is the search for useful and interesting supplementary materials that present historical events in a context that can be easily understood. The volumes in Lucent Books' World History Series attempt to present a broad, balanced, and penetrating view of the march of history. Ancient Egypt's important wars and rulers, for example, are presented against the rich and colorful backdrop of Egyptian religious, social, and cultural developments. The series engages the reader by enhancing historical events with these cultural contexts. For example, in *Ancient Greece*, the text covers the role of women in that society. Slavery is discussed in *The Roman Empire*, as well as how slaves earned their freedom. The numerous and varied aspects of everyday life in these and other societies are explored in each volume of the series. Additionally, the series covers the major political, cultural, and philosophical ideas as the torch of civilization is passed from ancient Mesopotamia and Egypt, through Greece, Rome, Medieval Europe, and other world cultures, to the modern day.

The material in the series is formatted in a thorough, precise, and organized manner. Each volume offers the reader a comprehensive and clearly written overview of an important historical event or period. The topic under discussion is placed in a broad historical context. For example, *The Italian Renaissance* begins with a discussion of the High Middle Ages and the loss of central control that allowed certain Italian cities to develop artistically. The book ends by looking forward to the Reformation and interpreting the societal changes that grew out of the Renaissance. Thus, students are not only involved in a historical era, but also enveloped by the events leading up to that era and the events following it.

One important and unique feature in the World History Series is the primary and secondary source quotations that richly supplement each volume. These quotes are useful in a number of ways. First, they allow students access to sources they would not normally be exposed to because of the difficulty and obscurity of the original source. The quotations range from interesting anecdotes to farsighted cultural perspectives and are drawn from historical witnesses both past and present. Second, the quotes demonstrate how and where historians themselves derive their information on the past as they strive to reach a consensus on historical events. Lastly, all of the quotes are footnoted, familiarizing students with the citation process and allowing them to verify quotes and/or look up the original source if the quote piques their interest.

Finally, the books in the World History Series provide a detailed launching point for further research. Each book contains a bibliography specifically geared toward student research. A second, annotated bibliography introduces students to all the sources the author consulted when compiling the book. A chronology of important dates gives students an overview, at a glance, of the topic covered. Where applicable, a glossary of terms is included.

In short, the series is designed not only to acquaint readers with the basics of history, but also to make them aware that their lives are a part of an ongoing human saga. Perhaps they will then come to the same realization as famed historian Arnold Toynbee. In his monumental work, *A Study of History,* he wrote about becoming aware of history flowing through him in a mighty current, and of his own life "welling like a wave in the flow of this vast tide."

Important Dates in the History of the Persian Empire

B.C. 3100	2700	2300	1900	1500	1100	700

B.C.

ca. 3100–2000
The Sumerian culture dominates the river valleys of Mesopotamia.

ca. 1100–1000
Aryan nomads from central Asia, the ancestors of the Medes and Persians, descend into Iran.

ca. 885
Assyria begins its rapid rise to power over much of the Near East.

625
Cyaxares II ascends the Median throne and begins expanding and reorganizing his army.

612
A combined force of Medes and Babylonians sacks Assyria's capital of Nineveh, causing the Assyrian Empire to collapse.

ca. 599
Persia's Cyrus II, later called "the Great," is born.

558
Cyrus II ascends the Persian throne.

550
After three years of fighting, Cyrus seizes Media's capital, Ecbatana, and takes control of the Median Empire.

546
Cyrus invades Lydia and captures its capital, Sardis, after which he subdues the Greek cities of Ionia, the region bordering the Aegean Sea; this marks the first important contact between Persians and Greeks.

539
Babylon falls to Cyrus's army, bringing the lands of the Babylonian Empire into the Persian fold.

525
Cyrus's son and successor, Cambyses II, invades and seizes Egypt.

522
In March, an impostor claiming to be Bardiya, Cyrus's younger son, whom Cambyses had previously killed, steals the throne; soon afterward Cambyses dies under mysterious circumstances; in September, a group of Persian nobles kill the impostor and install Darius I as king.

512
Darius crosses the Bosporus and enters Europe.

499–498
The Ionian Greek cities rebel, aided by small fleets from the mainland Greek cities of Athens and Eretria.

490
A Persian army crosses the Aegean; the invaders capture Eretria and deport its surviving inhabitants; a few weeks later, the Persians suffer an embarrassing defeat at the hands of a much smaller force of Athenian and Plataean hoplites on the plain of Marathon, northeast of Athens.

486
Darius dies and is succeeded by his son Xerxes.

480
Xerxes bridges the Hellespont and invades Greece with a huge army; an allied Greek fleet decisively defeats the Persian fleet in the bay of Salamis, southwest of Athens, and Xerxes retires to Sardis, leaving his general, Mardonius, to carry on the war.

479
Mardonius's army is annihilated by an allied Greek force near Plataea; the Persians

temporarily abandon the attempt to invade Europe.

465

Xerxes is assassinated by a group of conspirators; his son Artaxerxes I succeeds him.

424

After a long, largely undistinguished reign, Artaxerxes dies; a power struggle ensues from which a new king, Darius II, emerges.

404

Darius dies; after another bloody power struggle, his son Artaxerxes II ascends the throne.

401

Cyrus the Younger, the new king's brother, rebels; Cyrus leads a large army, including several thousand Greek mercenaries, to Cunaxa, near Babylon, and is there defeated by the king; the Greeks begin a harrowing, bloody retreat through Asia toward the Black Sea.

358

Artaxerxes is succeeded by his son Artaxerxes III.

338

One of the king's advisers, Bagoas, murders him and

places young Prince Arses on the throne; Philip II, king of the Greek kingdom of Macedonia, defeats the major Greek city-states and becomes master of Greece.

336

Arses is slain by Bagoas, who then crowns an obscure member of the Achaemenid family as Darius III; in Greece, Philip is assassinated and succeeded by his son, Alexander III, later called "the Great."

334

Alexander crosses the Hellespont and invades Persia.

331

After defeating two Persian armies and liberating Egypt, Alexander defeats Darius at Gaugamela, near the Tigris River; Darius flees and several months later dies at the hands of his own officers.

323

Alexander dies unexpectedly after completing his conquest of Persia; his leading generals almost immediately begin fighting over his realm; by 280, they have carved out three large kingdoms, including the Seleucid, which encompasses

large sections of the old Persian Empire.

238

Iranian nomads establish the Parthian dynasty; by 141, Parthia has replaced Seleucia as the major power in Iran and Mesopotamia.

A.D.
224

The last Parthian king is overthrown and the Sassanian dynasty takes control of the region.

637–651

Arab armies defeat the Sassanians and introduce Islamic religion and customs into Iran.

1941

Muhammad Reza Shah Pahlavi becomes shah of Iran; in the 1960s, he initiates an ambitious modernization program and in 1971 celebrates the 2,500th anniversary of the Achaemenid monarchy at the tomb of Cyrus the Great.

1979

In the wake of increasing social and religious unrest in Iran, the shah is replaced by an anti-Western Islamic republic under Ayatollah Khomeini.

The Villains of the Piece?

"It is shameful for us," stated the Greek orator Isocrates in 380 B.C., "who in our private life think the barbarians are fit only to be used as household slaves, to permit by our public policy so many of our allies to be enslaved by them."[1] The ancient Greeks commonly referred to all non-Greeks as barbarians; but in this case Isocrates specifically meant the Persians, whose empire, then the largest in human history, stretched from Asia Minor (what is now Turkey) in the west to the borders of India in the east. The remark was part of one of the orator's many calls for the nearly always warring Greek city-states to unite in an anti-Persian military crusade. The Persians were cowardly, asserted Isocrates, as well as effeminate (unmanly) and militarily incompetent. Therefore, the Greeks would have little trouble subduing them.

Isocrates was not alone in his contempt for the Persians. His contemporary, the famous Athenian philosopher Aristotle, held that barbarians, the Persians prominently among them, were "natural slaves." In his *Politics*, Aristotle writes:

It is undeniable that there are people who are slaves wherever they are, and others who are never and nowhere slaves. The same applies to noble birth; our nobles regard themselves as well born, not only in their own country but anywhere in the world; barbarians, however, are well born only in their own country.[2]

From this supposition, the philosopher concluded that it was perfectly natural for Greeks to rule over barbarians, but decidedly *un*natural for barbarians to rule over Greeks; and when he became tutor to Macedonia's prince Alexander, later called "the Great," about 342 B.C., he passed on to the boy a strong anti-Persian prejudice. Less than a decade later, as Alexander launched the invasion that would eventually bring Persia to its knees, his teacher's words were still fresh in his mind.

The low opinion most Greeks of that era held of their eastern neighbors was born of more than a century of distrust, enmity, and intermittent warfare between the two peoples. Bad relations stretched back to the years directly following the establishment of the Persian Empire by King Cyrus the Great, first prominent ruler of the royal Achaemenid dynasty, in the mid–sixth century B.C. Cyrus had conquered the Greek cities along the Aegean coast of Asia Minor, an area the Greeks called Ionia, and in the early fifth century the Persian monarchs Darius and Xerxes had invaded mainland Greece itself. The Greeks had managed to repel these attacks, but hatred, intrigue, and bloodshed between Greeks and Persians had continued on and off for another century. Not surprisingly, by Isocrates' and Aristotle's day nearly all Greeks had come to view the Persians as traditional mortal enemies, and the idea of an all-out crusade against Persia seemed both justified and compelling.

Greeks and Persians Inextricably Linked

Because the histories and destinies of the Greeks and Persians were so completely intertwined for over two centuries, it is impossible for modern historians and students to consider the history and culture of one of these peoples without considering the other. Unfortunately, in the case of the Persians this process is almost always hindered by the fact that the vast majority of surviving ancient historical sources about Persia were written by Greeks. The most fulsome and reliable of these is the fifth-century B.C. historian Herodotus's history of the Greek and Persian conflicts up to his own time. Other Greek writers whose books contain information about Persian history and culture include Xenophon (fourth century B.C.), Diodorus Siculus (first century B.C.), Plutarch (first century A.D.), and Arrian (second century A.D.).

Cyrus I, "the Great," who ruled Persia from 550 to 530 B.C., gave himself the title of "king of the Medes and Persians." He based his right to this title not only on conquest, but also on heritage, for supposedly his mother's father was the great Median king Astyages.

A Distorted View

By contrast, most surviving Persian sources discovered prior to the twentieth century consisted of carved stone reliefs, inscriptions chiseled into tombs or the sides of cliffs, and baked clay tablets bearing administrative records. With few exceptions, these yielded sketchy information about such topics as the lineages of kings and nobles, important military campaigns, and large-scale building projects, and barely hinted at lesser historical events or the customs, beliefs, and everyday lives of ordinary people. As a result, modern reconstructions of ancient Persia, at least until the early to mid-1900s, tended to be seen almost exclusively through Greek eyes. As the late great scholar of Persian culture A. T. Olmstead put it:

> The majority of available sources on Achaemenid history were in Greek. . . . The natural consequence was that the history of the mighty Achaemenid Empire was presented [in most Western history texts] as a series of uncorrelated episodes which found unity and significance only when inserted into the story of the little Greek states.[3]

Inevitably, such inadequate knowledge and coverage of Persian culture, combined with the strong anti-Persian bias of the Greek sources, led to a distorted, two-dimensional view of the Persians. For the most part, Western literature and art have tended to perpetuate the stereotypes created by men like Herodotus and Isocrates. Modern novels, movies, and even many histories have cast the Persians as the "villains of the piece," portraying Persia as a big, bad, autocratic, yet consistently incompetent bully bent on trying to crush the freedom-loving Greeks. These largely erroneous images only served to strengthen the ancient racist and ethnocentric prejudices that survived into modern times—biases that inevitably pictured Western cultures as inherently virtuous and vigorous, and their Eastern counterparts as sinister and corrupt.

When these biases are discounted, a much more positive portrait of ancient Persia emerges. Although several of Persia's leaders were indeed corrupt and ineffective, some, like Cyrus the Great and Darius I, were strong, generally wise and creative rulers who often tempered the wielding of absolute power with just and humane acts. And their huge empire was rich not only in natural resources and material goods but also in a cultural diversity that made it, in its own way, just as vigorous as Greece. Unlike Greek leaders, who ruled mainly Greeks, all of whom shared a single language and basic heritage, the ancient Persian monarchs commanded the allegiance and controlled the destinies of dozens of separate peoples, each with a peculiar ethnic heritage, language, and set of customs and religious beliefs. Because Persia consisted of a conglomeration of foreigners working together for the greater good, it was much more open to foreign and new ideas than was Greece. In this respect, Persia was more like the modern United States, whose strength derives in large degree from its cultural diversity.

The more rounded and realistic portrait of ancient Persia that has begun to emerge in recent decades rests partly on a fresh, more impartial reassessment of the old Greek texts, but to a greater degree on new archaeological discoveries. The first methodical excavations of the great Persian palace at Persepolis (destroyed by Alexander in the 320s B.C.) took place in the early 1930s; in the years that followed, this and other Persian sites produced more artifacts and clay tablets. From some of these finds, Olmstead points out,

> we may learn the names of the workmen [who built the palaces] and the countries from which they came, the work which they did, and the salaries they were paid. We learn, too, of a new daughter of Darius named after a mother whom we knew already, and of a gift with which she was provided. . . . From the minor archaeological findings and from the tablets, we obtain for the first time some idea of the life of the common people.[4]

New twenty-first-century excavations and studies will undoubtedly reveal much more about ancient Persia, one of the most powerful and splendid empires in world history. True, its age of greatest power and glory lasted for just over two centuries, not long when compared with, for instance, that of ancient Rome, which was a major power for more than seven hundred years. But consider that the Persian Empire's life span was about equal to that of the United States from its birth in 1776 to the present. Americans often look back proudly on what they see as a long, complex, and dramatic history of cultural, military, and artistic achievement that irrevocably changed the world; and in their own time, the Persians were justified in doing the same.

Chapter

1 The Ancient Near East: A Crossroads of Cultures

At its height, the ancient Persian Empire spanned most of the region now referred to as the Near East (or Middle East), stretching from the Mediterranean coast in the west to the borders of India in the east. More specifically, Persia's heartland encompassed the area occupied today by the nation of Iran. The central portion of this geographically diverse region consists of the massive Iranian plateau, which, at an average elevation of three thousand to six thousand feet above sea level, stretches some six hundred miles from the Caspian Sea in the north to the Persian Gulf in the south. Marking the region's eastern extremity are two great salt deserts, the Dasht-e-Kavīr and the Dasht-e-Lūt; to the west, the towering, rugged Zagros Mountains run diagonally along the plateau from the northwest to the southeast; and west of these often snowcapped peaks, the plateau rapidly drops away into the flat alluvial plains of the valley of the Tigris and Euphrates Rivers, an area long known as Mesopotamia.[5]

Long before the rise of Persia, the Near East's great diversity of terrain and climate, along with its strategic location, made it highly attractive to settlement and it naturally became a great crossroads of cultures. As early as the fourth millennium B.C., and probably even earlier, the area had already begun to receive periodic migrations of peoples, particularly from the steppes ringing the Caspian Sea in the north. These groups both contributed to the region's ethnic and cultural diversity and benefited from its increasing prosperity. The first political units to appear were independent city-states, each consisting of an urban center surrounded by supporting villages and farmland. In time, groups of these small states coalesced into nations; and some of these, in turn, eventually became aggressive, amassed large armies, and conquered their neighbors, creating the first empires. This set in motion a pattern of increasing military and political expansion that would eventually culminate in the largest native empire the Near East would ever see—that of Persia.

A Series of Successful Peoples

Like many other Near Eastern peoples, the Persians inherited a large proportion of their political, military, and cultural ideas from the highly successful civilizations that grew up along the Tigris and Euphrates Rivers. With its abundance of water and fertile soil, Mesopotamia was one of the first Near Eastern regions (a second being Egypt) to develop widespread agriculture, trade routes, and city-states. From about 3100 to 2000 B.C., the area was dominated by dynasties, city-states, and small empires collectively referred to as Sumerian, after the city of Sumer, located near the Persian Gulf in what is now southeastern Iraq. Over time the Sumerians were absorbed by other peoples, most notably the Babylonians, whose capital, Babylon, rose on the Euphrates about three hundred miles northwest of the Gulf. Succeeding Babylonian dynasties controlled Mesopotamia for the next thousand years. Historian Chester Starr describes how these peoples lived:

By canals and by roads the countryside was divided into relatively regular plots which were defined by geometrical means. Farmers employed wooden plows, seed-drills, and stone hoes to reap 40-fold returns of barley; shepherds and dogs watched flocks of sheep and goats; other areas were gardens with mudbrick walls, set about with fruit trees and overshadowed by date palms. Asses on the paths and boats on the canals carried the rich products of the fields to the vital hubs, the cities. Each city . . . was girdled by a moat and a wall of sun-dried brick. . . . Within the gates, where a regular guard of soldiers watched traffic, streets wide enough for chariots and wagons ran between blocks of houses of the well-to-do; behind these were alleys and great masses of small, flat-roofed huts. Here lived mostly the farmers, who trudged out every day to the fields (though some lived in subsidiary mudbrick villages) . . . [and] there were also smiths, potters, and the like.[6]

The successful Sumerians and Babylonians spread their influence over neighboring Near Eastern peoples, including the then less culturally advanced inhabitants

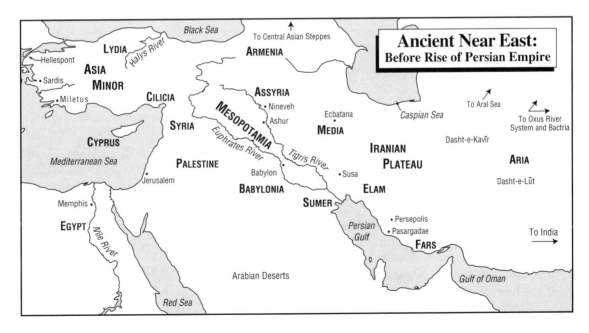

Ancient Near East:
Before Rise of Persian Empire

of the Iranian plateau. The first major Iranian culture, the Elamite, emerged in the third millennium B.C. Elam roughly encompassed the plateau's southern highlands, a region known as Fars (also Pars or Parsa), as well as the nearby lowland areas bordering the Persian Gulf, including the important city of Susa. For a long time the Elamites were dominated by the Sumerians. But by the beginning of the second millennium, with Sumer having declined, Elam became an independent state. The Elamites reached their cultural and political zenith between 1450 and 1125 B.C., a period in which they carved inscriptions in their unique language, produced exquisite artifacts of gold, silver, and bronze, and in general enjoyed great prosperity.

Elam's heyday came to an abrupt end, however, when the Babylonians, under Nebuchadrezzar I, invaded in the last decades of the twelfth century B.C. In the four centuries that followed, southern and western Iran felt the influence not only of Babylon, but of several other foreign masters, the most powerful of whom were the Assyrians. Taking its name from the city of Ashur, on the banks of the northern Tigris, Assyria existed as a minor Mesopotamian state through most of the second millennium B.C. Then, in the ninth century B.C. the Assyrians, led by a series of vigorous and warlike kings, suddenly burst outward from their small homeland and began carving out a huge empire. By the 660s B.C. this realm, the largest in the Near East up to that time, included much of the Iranian plateau in the east, Babylonia and the rest of Mesopotamia in the center, and Syria, Palestine, and parts of Egypt in the west. Credit for the Assyrians' success goes in part to their large, fearsome army and to their brutally efficient methods of seizing and ruling foreign lands. According to scholar D. J. Wiseman:

> Assyrian methods were harsh, designed to inflict a lesson of "frightfulness" upon the peoples who transgressed the bounds set by their god. Those who failed to flee were killed,

The ruins of an ancient Elamite town. Among the artifacts discovered in Elamite remains are attractive pottery vessels dubbed "kaftari ware" by archaeologists; these are usually buff-colored and decorated with rows of birds.

Attempts to Date the Iranian Migration

Historians remain unsure about the exact time of the Aryan migrations that brought the ancestors of the Persians into Iran. In this excerpt from his book Ancient Persia, *scholar John Curtis explains how pottery types, in particular a type known as Early Western Gray Ware that appeared in northwestern Iran in the late second millennium* B.C., *might provide clues.*

"It is sometimes thought that the appearance of this gray ware pottery in western Iran signifies the first arrival there of the Iranians, forbears of the . . . Medes and Persians. They are mentioned first during the reign of the Assyrian king Shalmaneser III (858–824 B.C.), who campaigned in western Iran. It is supposed that these people, who spoke Indo-European languages, were not indigenous to Iran—their homeland is thought to have been somewhere in the vast expanse of steppeland that stretched from the river Danube east to the Ural Mountains. . . . The Iron Age gray wares of western Iran appear to be derived from the earlier Late Bronze Age gray wares found at sites . . . near the southeast corner of the Caspian Sea. At sites in western Iran where gray ware has been found there is a sudden break from earlier pottery traditions, and . . . these facts could indicate that people using gray ware pottery arrived in western Iran from the east. . . . It is possible, therefore, that the Iranians . . . spread into western Iran in the second half of the second millennium B.C. This is an attractive theory, but the issue is extremely complex. . . . We have no idea of the numbers of people involved in this projected migration, nor do we know anything about how they traveled or what social structure they had. The exact date of their arrival in western Iran may never be satisfactorily resolved; indeed, it is possible that the migration took place over a long period of time, perhaps even extending to many centuries."

their villages sacked and their crops fired. Gradually the new areas overrun were forced to pay an initial tribute followed by annual payments to ensure good behavior. In this way great quantities of booty were taken, with the emphasis on rare materials and potential war weapons, including horses and other animals. The Assyrians came to rely on this as a source of luxuries which supplemented their economy. The ruler of the raided area was forced to agree [to] terms of a loyalty-treaty enforceable under oath

This bas-relief from the palace of Ashurbanipal shows a heavy royal war chariot manned by a crew of four and supported by a mounted archer in front. Some smaller and lighter Assyrian chariots were more flexible because they could be dismantled and carried over rough terrain.

which invoked the wrath of the Assyrian gods on any infringement. This provided the religious and legal sanction for any subsequent Assyrian intervention as well as a strong incentive for the vassal not to repeat any misdemeanor. . . . As one means of control the Assyrians left behind a local official, backed by a small garrison or guard, to report on the local situation and on any subversive activity. These intelligence reports were sent in by messengers and often alerted the Assyrians in time to take remedial action in concert with loyal vassals.[7]

The Rise of Media

But even before the Assyrian kings spread their harsh rule over large sections of the Near East, the seeds of their destruction had been planted in the uplands of the Iranian plateau. The periodic migrations of nomadic peoples from the central Asian steppes had continued through the second millennium, and perhaps sometime between 1100 and 1000 B.C. (the exact date is much disputed) small groups identifying themselves as Aryans descended onto the plateau. The name Iran, which later came to identify the region, is derived from the word *aryanam*, meaning "land of the Aryans." Surviving Assyrian annals reveal that by the mid–ninth

Assyrian warriors ruthlessly impale prisoners who were captured during a raid into Palestine.

Assyria's Deadly Chariots

One of the keys to the success of the fearsome Assyrian army was its efficient use of war chariots, as described here (from an essay published in Warfare in the Ancient World*) by the distinguished Assyriologist D. J. Wiseman.*

"The principal strength of the Assyrian army lay in its chariotry. This mobile weapons-platform was in use in the area of the northern [Mesopotamian] plains during the 13th–12th centuries B.C. and then developed . . . to combine the skilled employment of horses with a specially constructed vehicle. Chariots of the 9th century were sometimes drawn by a team of four horses but their clumsiness and vulnerability led to their abandonment as war vehicles. Changes in technology enabled ironsmiths to design a light vehicle with a wooden frame set on a metal undercarriage with the wheel axis moved back from the center to the rear. The result was a highly maneuverable vehicle which required less traction effort. . . . The chariot's driver was held steady against the front screen while the rigid shaft, originally elliptical but later straight, made control of the two yoked horses easier. The car became increasingly rectangular in shape to accommodate more armor and crew. . . . On the approach to battle an additional or spare horse was hitched to the rear. The light chariot was usually manned by a crew of two, the driver and an archer or lancer, but after the 9th century a third man was added to strengthen rear defense with one or more shields. . . . Chariotry was employed either in shock action in the center of the attack, a tactic which greatly reduced the value of massed infantry in open battle, or on the wings in encircling maneuvers in concert with the cavalry."

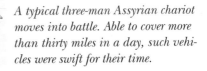

A typical three-man Assyrian chariot moves into battle. Able to cover more than thirty miles in a day, such vehicles were swift for their time.

century B.C. two Aryan peoples were well established; the Mada, whom we call the Medes, settled mainly in the northwestern portion of the plateau around the city of Ecbatana (modern Hamadan), and the Parsua, the Persians, eventually occupied the old Elamite land of Fars.

The Medes were the first of these two new Iranian peoples to gain military and political prominence in Near Eastern affairs. They were apparently strong enough by the mid-700s B.C. to pose at least a moderate threat to the Assyrians, whose annals record two Median campaigns, led by King Tiglath Pileser III (reigned 744–727) and King Sargon (reigned 721–705), respectively. Assyrian carved reliefs from this era depict Median fortresses with high battlements equipped with notches through which defenders could hurl missile weapons at attackers. Reflecting their unpolished nomadic roots, the Medes themselves appear on these reliefs, according to Olmstead's description,

> with short hair confined by a red fillet [band of material] and with short curled beard; over a tunic is worn the sheepskin coat, still the traveler's best friend in the bitter winter of the plateau, which also required high-laced boots to plow through the deep snows. They were armed with only the long spear and were defended by the rectangular wicker shield.[8]

The Medes also employed archers on horseback, a military practice inherited from their ancestors, the nomads of the central Asian steppes.[9]

Undaunted by Assyrian aggression, the Medes grew stronger. This trend culminated in the accession in 625 B.C. of Cyaxares II, the dynamic ruler who was destined finally to defeat the Assyrians and in the process launch the Median Empire. The key to Cyaxares' success was evidently his program of military expansion and reorganization, which he instituted immediately after succeeding his father, Phraortes. Cyaxares organized his spearmen, archers, and cavalry into distinct units, each of which was trained separately for a specific use on the battlefield. He also instituted standardized military uniforms, consisting of a long-sleeved leather tunic that ended above the knee, held by a double belt with a round buckle; leather trousers; laced shoes with projecting tips; and on the head a round felt cap with a neck flap. Archers, and also some soldiers who used both spear and bow, carried their bows in very elaborate cases and kept their arrows in leather quivers that hung from the shoulder or waist. Although many of Cyaxares' troops were native Medes, he also drew recruits from minor Iranian peoples whom Media held as vassals, or dependents who exchanged their allegiance for the protection of the stronger power; sometime during the early part of his reign, the Persians in Fars also became Median vassals.

The Fall of Assyria

When Cyaxares was confident that his army was sufficiently large and formidable, he laid his plans for an assault on the Assyrians. He knew that Assyria, once the scourge of the Near East, had lately been weakened in squelching numerous rebellions by its subject peoples and was therefore vulnerable. Nevertheless, he rea-

Not long after assuming the Median throne, King Cyaxares II (on horseback) rallies his countrymen to defend their land from invaders. Note the typical Median felt caps.

soned, it would be foolhardy to take the enemy too lightly; so he wisely made an alliance with Babylonia's king Nabopolassar, who hated the Assyrians as much as he did. About 614 the combined Median-Babylonian forces poured into the Assyrian homeland on the upper reaches of the Tigris. Town after town fell to the invaders until finally, in 612, they stormed what was then Assyria's largest and most important city, Nineveh. The Hebrew prophet Nahum, a contemporary of Cyaxares, gives this vivid description of the city's bloody fall:

The shatterer [Cyaxares? Nabopolassar? the hand of God?] has come up against you. Man the ramparts . . . collect all your strength. . . . The shield of his mighty men is red, his soldiers are clothed in scarlet. The chariots flash like flame when mustered in array; the chargers prance. The chariots rage in the streets, they rush to and fro through the squares; they gleam like torches, they dart like lightning. . . . The river gates are opened, the palace is in dismay; its mistress [the queen?] is stripped, she is carried off, her

A depiction of the fabled hanging gardens of Babylon, built by King Nebuchadrezzar II for his Median bride, Amytis.

maidens lamenting. . . . Nineveh is like a pool whose waters run away. "Halt! Halt!" they cry; but none turns back. Plunder the silver, plunder the gold! There is no end of treasure, or wealth of every precious thing. Desolate! Desolation and ruin! Hearts faint and knees tremble, anguish is on all loins, all faces grow pale! . . . Woe to the bloody city, all full of lies and booty—no end to the plunder! The crack of the whip, the rumble of the wheel, galloping horse and bounding chariot! Horsemen charging, flashing sword and glittering spear, hosts of slain, heaps of corpses, dead bodies without end—they stumble over the bodies![10]

The campaign against Assyria was so successful that its once mighty empire

quickly shattered; thereafter, all that remained of the Assyrians was the memory of their cruelty.[11] The Medes and Babylonians divided the Assyrian lands and for a time coexisted in peace. Nabopolassar's son, Nebuchadrezzar II, who ascended the Babylonian throne in 605, helped to cement the grand alliance by marrying a Median princess, Amytis. It was for her that he built the famous hanging gardens of Babylon, later named one of the seven wonders of the ancient world. In addition to bringing together the Medes and Babylonians, the destruction of Assyria created a new balance of power in the Near East, in which four nations of roughly the same strength dominated the landscape. Besides Media and Babylonia (sometimes referred to as Chaldea because Nabopolassar, who hailed from Chaldea, a small province on the northern coast of the Persian Gulf, had established the so-called Chaldean dynasty), these powers included Lydia, which occupied most of Asia Minor, and Egypt.

Darkness at Noon

But Cyaxares was not content to maintain this balance of power. Like so many other successful kings and military leaders in history, he dreamed of expanding his realm at the expense of his neighbors; and not long after consolidating the former northern Assyrian lands, he began a series of foreign conquests. After much hard fighting, the Medes subjugated the Cadusii, who inhabited the thick woodlands on the southern border of the Caspian Sea. Cyaxares also struck westward and by 590 had captured Armenia, the mountainous region nestled between Asia Minor and the Caspian.

Convinced that these aggressions had made him stronger, Cyaxares apparently did not foresee the serious problems he faced in maintaining a far-flung empire.

Among these were the purely logistical difficulties of communication and transportation of soldiers and supplies over long distances. Potentially more dangerous was the constant threat of rebellion by discontented subject peoples, for the

The Fabulous Hanging Gardens

In this tract from his Library of History, *the first-century B.C. Greek historian Diodorus Siculus describes the famous hanging gardens of Babylon, which number among the seven wonders of the ancient world.*

"There was also, beside the acropolis [central fortress], the Hanging Garden, as it is called, which was built . . . by a later [Babylonian] king to please one of his concubines; for she, they say, being a Persian by race [Diodorus here confuses Persia with Media] and longing for the meadows of her mountains, asked the king to imitate, through the artifice of a planted garden, the distinctive landscape of Persia. . . . Since the approach to the garden sloped like a hillside and the several parts of the structure rose from one another tier on tier, the appearance of the whole resembled that of a theater. When the ascending terraces had been built, there had been constructed beneath them galleries which carried the entire weight of the planted garden and rose little by little one above the other. . . . The roofs of the galleries were covered over with beams of stone sixteen foot long. . . . The roof above these beams had first a layer of reeds laid in great quantities of bitumen [tar], over this two courses of baked brick bonded by cement, and as a third layer a covering of lead, to the end that the moisture from the soil might not penetrate beneath. On all this again the earth had been piled to the depth sufficient for the roots of the largest trees; and the ground . . . was thickly planted with trees of every kind. . . . And since the galleries . . . all received the light, they contained many royal lodges of every description; and there was one gallery which contained openings leading from . . . machines for supplying the gardens with water, the machines raising the water in great abundance from the river."

Median Empire was a conglomeration of vassal states inhabited by different races and cultures, all of whom resented the Medes and had to be held together by force. Further complicating matters was the fact that Media's native language and customs were not distinctive or attractive enough for the conquered peoples to find worthy of adoption. As historian Alessandro Bausani puts it:

It does not appear that the Medes had a strong culture of their own since, in the monumental inscriptions of the Persian kings after the unification of the states of Media and Persia, it was found necessary to use the Elamite and Babylonian languages but not the Median, which therefore probably did not possess a script and furthermore was not too dissimilar from Persian. Also the customs of the Median kings seemed to have been modeled on those of the Babylonians and Assyrians.[12]

Confident that he could maintain the foreign territories he had acquired and desirous of obtaining more, in about 589 Cyaxares moved westward from Armenia and invaded one of the other great powers, Lydia. The Lydian king, Alyattes, met the challenge with his own formidable army and, according to Herodotus, the war "continued for five years during which both Lydians and Medes won a number of victories." But it was natural rather than human forces that brought the conflict to a sudden and unexpected halt. In one of history's greatest accidents of timing, on May 28, 585, at the height of a great battle between the opposing forces, a total eclipse of the sun occurred. Herodotus later recorded:

After five years of indecisive warfare, a battle took place in which the armies had already engaged when day was suddenly turned into night. This change from daylight to darkness had been foretold to the Ionians [then subjects of Lydia; some of these Greeks probably fought in Alyattes' army] by [the Greek scientist] Thales of Miletus, who fixed the date for it in the year in which it did, in fact, take place. Both Lydians and Medes broke off the engagement when they saw this darkening of the day.[13]

Believing this frightening onset of darkness at noon to be an omen of ill fortune, Cyaxares marched his troops out of Lydia, never to return. He died the following year, unaware that the eclipse would indeed prove a portent of bad luck for the Medes; for their short-lived empire would itself soon be eclipsed by one of their own subject peoples, a group closely related in language and cultural heritage. The Persians were about to make their unexpected and stunning entrance onto history's grand stage.

2 A Man of Vision and Talent: Cyrus the Great Builds an Empire

When Cyrus II, the Persian Empire's founder and greatest king, was born in about 599 B.C., his world was already ancient. Over long, tumultuous centuries the great empires of Mesopotamia and Iran had risen and fallen like an endless tide, leaving the crumbling ruins of both cities and human ambition in their wake. The newest incoming wave in this historical tide, Media, was growing ever stronger; Cyrus was barely ten when Cyaxares' army swept through Armenia and then spun westward to conquer Lydia. At the time, the boy could not have guessed that Media's seemingly unstoppable wave would only briefly crest and then suddenly collapse, or that he himself would be the chief cause of its untimely end.

Nor could young Cyrus have dreamed that he and the members of his own family line would create the greatest imperial wave ever to sweep over the Near East. The boy traced his lineage back to Achaemenes, the semilegendary founder of the Persian royal family who, it was said, had molded the rude hill tribes of Fars into a small nation. That proud nation now languished in vassal status under the ambitious Medes; but this situation was not destined to endure. As Cyrus grew to become a man of remarkable vision, courage, and talent, he would not only free his people from Median domination, but in an amazingly short time raise the Achaemenid dynasty to a position of unsurpassed power and influence over much of the known world. Alessandro Bausani comments:

> The sudden rise and assertion of power of the Persians under . . . Cyrus the Great . . . is one of those astonishing

A fanciful modern depiction of Cyrus II, Persia's first and greatest king.

but not infrequent phenomena in the history of Asia past or present. It shows how a tiny state can, for no apparent reason, trigger off an explosion like that of a new star, widely extending its boundaries to include many peoples of various races.[14]

Media's Sudden Fall

Cyrus ascended the Persian throne in 558 at the age of about forty-one. With an astute sense of human nature and a strong grasp of the international political forces of his day, he must have already been aware that many of the Median nobles under Astyages, Cyaxares' successor, were unhappy with their new king. Astyages, far from the vigorous and capable ruler Cyaxares had been, apparently spent much of his time indulging in the various excesses of the newly sumptuous Median court at Ecbatana. Cyrus also realized that the Median Empire's subject peoples, most of whom were obliged to contribute soldiers to its army, were even more discontented and might give Astyages little support if he was attacked.

Having studied his enemies' weaknesses, Cyrus steadily drew his plans against them, striking his first blow in 553. Few details are known about the Persian rebellion beyond that it ended three years later with Cyrus marching directly on Media's capital of Ecbatana. According to Herodotus:

Astyages thereupon armed the Medes to a man. . . . When they took the field and engaged the Persian army, a few . . . did their duty, but of the remain-

This stone stele dedicated to Cyrus is among the few relics left standing in the ruins of his palace at Pasargadae.

der some deserted to the Persians and the greater number deliberately shirked fighting and took to their heels. When Astyages learned of the disgraceful collapse of the Median army, he swore that even so Cyrus should not get away with it so easily; then . . . he armed all Medes, both under and over military age, who had been left in the city, led them out to battle and was defeated. His men were killed and he himself was taken alive.[15]

Thus did the only recently formed Median Empire come to a sudden and disastrous end at Cyrus's hands. Yet Media itself was not destroyed. Displaying the wisdom and leniency of a great ruler, Cyrus honored the Medes, giving many of their nobles high positions in his court and generalships in his army. He made the Median homeland the first province, or satrapy, of his own empire, calling it Mada, and kept Ecbatana intact as his second capital, after Pasargadae in the hills of Fars; and thereafter, the Persian realm was routinely referred to as that of the "Medes and Persians." Cyrus also showed extraordinary mercy to his former enemy Astyages, treating him with consideration and allowing him to attend the royal court for the rest of his natural life. In these ways, Cyrus tempered his image as a military strongman with acts of civility and fairness and thereby gained the admiration and loyalty of his subjects.

Military and Political Organization

In conquering Media, Cyrus laid claim to all of the lands over which Astyages had ruled, including most of the former Assyrian homeland, mountainous Armenia, Syria on the Mediterranean coast, and large sections of the Iranian plateau. Perhaps inspired by what he believed to be Persia's divine destiny, or his own, he dreamed of further expanding this realm. But to do so, he realized, he would need the strongest and most flexible military and political systems the Near East had ever seen; and he worked diligently at developing and perfecting both throughout the remainder of his life.

Cyrus's military was modeled in large degree on that of the Assyrians, although he modified and improved their system. The Assyrians had made major and highly effective use of a tactical feature common in Near Eastern warfare for many centuries. This was the archer-pair, consisting of a spearman bearing a very large, light but sturdy shield made of leather and wicker, and an archer; the spearman faced the enemy and held up the shield, behind which the archer hid and fired off volleys of arrows. The Persians called such shields *spara* and so named these tactical units *sparabara*, or "shield-bearers." Typically,

Archers of the royal Persian guard adorn a brick-faced wall at the palace at Susa. Each man carries a curved bow, large quiver, spear, and also probably a dagger.

the Assyrians had lined these units up side by side, forming a single row of shield carriers backed by a single row of archers. Cyrus increased the depth of the formation and also the number of archers per shield, producing a heavier concentration of arrow shot.

The organization of these early Persian infantrymen followed the decimal system. As classical scholar Nick Sekunda explains:

> The Persian army was organized into regiments of a thousand men. The Old Persian term for one of these regiments was *hazarabam*. . . . Each regiment was commanded by a *hazarapatis*, or "commander of a thousand," and was divided into ten *sataba* of a hundred. Each *satabam* was commanded by a *satapatis* and was, in turn, divided into ten *dathaba* of ten men. The *dathabam* of ten formed the basic tactical sub-unit in the infantry, and was drawn up on the battlefield in file. The *dathapatis* was stationed in the front rank, carrying the *spara*. Behind him the rest of the *dathabam* would be drawn up in nine ranks, each man armed with a bow and falchion [curved sword]. Normally the *dathapatis* carried a short fighting-spear six feet long, and was expected to protect the rest of the *dathabam* should the enemy reach the line. Sometimes, however, the whole of the *dathabam* were armed with bows, and the *spara* were propped up as a "wall" at the front, allowing the entire *dathabam* to discharge projectiles.[16]

The use of the decimal system continued for units bigger than regiments. Large armies contained units composed of ten *hazaraba*, or ten thousand men; the Persian term for these large groups has been lost but the Greeks called them "myriads." The most important of the Persian myriads was the elite group that formed the king's personal bodyguard. The best soldiers in the army, they became known as the *Amrtaka*, or "Immortals," this name deriving from the practice of immediately replacing any of their number who died.

In addition to his infantry, Cyrus made use of other kinds of tactical units. At first he relied for his cavalry on regiments of Medes, the most highly skilled horsemen in the Near East; but over time he devel-

What Persian Soldiers Wore

In his Histories, *Herodotus supplied this thumbnail sketch of a Persian infantryman's attire.*

"The dress of these troops consisted of the tiara, or soft felt cap, embroidered tunic with sleeves, a coat of mail looking like the scales of a fish, and trousers; for arms they carried light wicker shields, quivers slung below them, short spears, powerful bows with cane arrows, and daggers swinging from belts beside the right thigh."

Cyrus (seated on throne) convenes a war council in one of his royal throne rooms. He based much of his military and political organization on Assyrian models, although he significantly improved on them.

oped an elite corps of mounted warriors drawn from the Persian nobility. He also employed an old Assyrian mainstay—war chariots—making significant improvements in their construction to make them more formidable in direct frontal assaults on enemy lines. According to the account of Cyrus's life written by the fourth-century B.C. Greek historian Xenophon:

> He had chariots of war constructed with strong wheels, so that they might not easily be broken, and with long axles; for anything broad is less likely to be overturned. The box for the driver he constructed out of strong timbers in the form of a turret; and this rose in height to the driver's elbows, so that they could manage the horses by reaching over the top of the box; and besides, he covered the drivers with mail [armor], all except their eyes. On both sides of the wheels, moreover, he attached to the axles steel scythes [blades] . . . with the intention of hurling the chariots into the midst of the enemy.[17]

In general, members of the infantry, cavalry, and chariotry were variously drawn from both the nobility and the commoners, for military service was compulsory for all Persian men. Every male between the ages of twenty and twenty-four was expected to train and/or fight, and many stayed in the service longer, sometimes until they were as old as fifty.

Cyrus also based the political organization of his empire on Assyrian models, once more making substantial improvements. The Assyrians had divided their realm into provinces, each administered by a governor who reported directly to the king in Nineveh. In a similar fashion, Cyrus created satrapies, each encompassing the geography and culture of a single conquered nation. The satrap, or "protector of the kingdom," who administered each satrapy wielded considerable power; so to counter the possibility of a satrap's threatening the king's central authority, Cyrus instituted effective checks. Although a satrap was allowed to command levies of local troops to police his province, his secretary, financial officer, and the leader of the royal military garrison in his capital all reported directly to the king. As an added measure, Cyrus maintained a network of spies to keep him informed of all important events occurring in distant reaches of the realm.

The Invasion of Lydia

Cyrus's strong military and political organization proved to be the key to his success as he began his methodical expansion of the empire he had usurped from the Medes. His defeat of Media had not only given him control of large foreign territories, but also upset the delicate balance of power in the Near East. The other three great powers—Egypt, Babylonia, and Lydia—looked on Cyrus as an upstart who posed a threat to their own security, an assessment that proved correct when he brazenly invaded Lydia in 546. Bent on demonstrating that he was a greater conqueror than Cyaxares, who, Cyrus believed, had abandoned Lydia too easily, Persia's Great King, less impressed by omens than the former Median leader, was not about to let fears of a mere eclipse stand in the way of his campaign of world conquest.

Ironically, belief in omens did play an important role in unfolding events when Cyrus entered Lydia, except that this time it was solely the new Lydian king, Croesus, Alyattes' son, who allowed superstition to guide his actions. Croesus greatly admired the Greeks, some of whom—the Ionians—were his subjects, and he faithfully followed many Greek customs. One of these was to consult the famous oracle at Delphi, a town in the central region of mainland Greece, at times of indecision or crisis. The oracle was a priestess who, it was widely believed, delivered divine advice and prophecies by acting as a medium between the gods and humans. Accordingly, Croesus sent a messenger to ask the oracle whether it would be wise to fight Cyrus. The oracle's answer was that if the Lydian king crossed the Halys River, in central Asia Minor, and attacked the Persians he would destroy a great empire. Thus filled with confidence, Croesus crossed the Halys and attacked, but to his surprise he was unable to defeat Cyrus's powerful army; after this indecisive engagement the Lydians retreated back to their capital of Sardis, located about fifty miles inland from the Aegean coast. Cyrus quickly followed and the armies met again. This time, as Herodotus later told it, it was

> on the level ground in front of Sardis; it is a broad expanse, bare of trees. . . . When Cyrus saw the Lydians take up battle positions on this plain, his fear of their cavalry [which at the time outnumbered his own] led him to adopt a suggestion of Harpagus, one of the Medes; this was to get together all the camels (they were used as pack-animals to carry equipment and stores), unload them and mount men armed as cavalrymen on their backs. He then ordered them to advance as the first line of attack against the cavalry of Croesus, with the infantry following and his own cavalry bringing up the rear. . . . The reason for confronting the Lydian cavalry with camels was the instinctive fear which they inspire in horses. . . . The ruse succeeded, for when the battle began, the horses turned tail the moment they saw and smelled the camels—and Croesus's chief ground of confidence was cut from under him. . . . Both sides suffered heavy losses, but finally the Lydians, forced to retire, were driven within the city walls, where they were besieged by the Persians.[18]

The oracle (the priestess swooning with hands upraised) of the famous shrine at Delphi delivers a prophecy to some eagerly awaiting religious pilgrims.

Effectively employing siege tactics, another military technique inherited largely from the Assyrians, Cyrus took Sardis and began to transform Lydia into another Persian satrapy. Croesus had accepted the Delphic oracle's prophecy and gone down to defeat; but as Herodotus points out, he could hardly blame the oracle for his misfortune, because

> the god had declared that if he attacked the Persians he would bring down a mighty empire. After an answer like that, the wise thing would have

Lydia's King Croesus was a great admirer of the Greeks. The Greek historian Herodotus penned several detailed anecdotes about this colorful ruler.

been to send again to inquire which empire was meant, Cyrus's or his own. But as he misinterpreted what was said and made no second inquiry, he must admit the fault to have been his own.[19]

Persia's First Contact with the Greeks

Lydia's fall, marking Cyrus's subjugation of a second of the former four great powers, sent shock waves throughout the Near East. The Persian victory also stunned the Ionian Greek cities on the Aegean coast, who now stood face-to-face with Cyrus's great war machine. In desperation, they appealed to Sparta, the city-state that dominated the Peloponnesus, the large peninsula that makes up the southern third of Greece. All Greeks feared and respected the small but formidable Spartan army, considered by most to be invincible. The Spartans were also renowned for their reluctance to stray far from home, however, and they did not send their army.[20] Instead, they dispatched a messenger to Cyrus with the bold warning that if the Persians dared to attack any Greek cities, Sparta would intervene.

To the mighty Persian king, who already ruled over roughly a quarter of the known world, the Greek city-states represented nothing more than a scattering of tiny backward villages on the fringes of civilization; he was aware, for instance, that the largest Greek states could field armies of no more than a few thousand troops, and most others only a few hundred. Therefore, he found the Spartan ultimatum both comical and insulting. He told the Spartan messenger: "I have never yet

Gathering Supplies for a Campaign

These excerpts from Xenophon's tribute to Cyrus, the Cyropaedia, *part of the long list of provisions the Persian king supposedly ordered collected for a campaign, reveal the kinds of supplies utilized by traveling armies of the period.*

"If anyone has a generous supply of clothing with him, that will be of good service to him whether he be well or ill. . . . We must take with us the things that sick people need; for the weight they add is very small and, if we have a case of sickness, they will be very necessary. We must also have plenty of straps; for nearly everything that men and horses have is fastened in with straps, and when these wear out or break, everything must come to a standstill. . . . We must also have a good supply of lumber for the chariots and the wagons, for from constant use many parts necessarily become defective. We must also have the most indispensable tools for all these purposes. . . . Besides these, we must have a shovel . . . for every wagon, and for each pack animal an ax and a sickle. . . . You superintendents of the engineering corps . . . are to march [your workers] in squads ahead of the wagons, so that, in case there is any need of road-building, you may get to work without delay. . . . I shall take along . . . smiths, carpenters, and cobblers . . . and they shall be relieved of assignments to duty, under arms, but . . . ply their trades for pay at the order of whoever wishes their services."

been afraid of men who have a special meeting place in the center of their city, where they swear this and that and chat with each other. Such people, if *I* have anything to do with it, will not have merely the troubles of Ionia to chatter about, but [also] their own."[21]

Having called Sparta's bluff, Cyrus proceeded to lay siege to the Ionian cities, who failed to unite against him. As he had fully anticipated, the tough-talking Spartans did nothing to aid their fellow Greeks, and soon the defeated Ionians had to endure the humiliation of paying Cyrus yearly tribute (gold and other valuables) and supplying soldiers for his army. This first major contact between Persia and Greece, whose relationship would in time profoundly affect both peoples, taught the Persians much about the Greeks. The Persians, says Olmstead,

learned that as individuals [the Greeks] were excellent fighters, clever and well armed, and worthy of incorporation into their own armies. They discovered

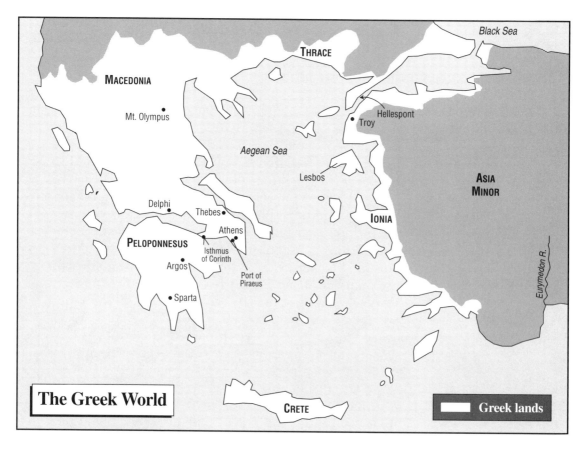

The Greek World

Greek lands

also that the Greek city-states, bitterly jealous of one another, were incapable of united action and that it was not difficult to find purchasable friends among them. . . . But the greatest discovery of all was that there were class divisions within the city-states themselves [and the Persians could, through bribery and other means, play one class against another].[22]

Cyrus Triumphant

After his successful conquests in the west, Cyrus returned to the Persian homeland in Fars and began the construction of palaces and other royal buildings at Pasargadae. Many of the stonemasons who worked on these projects were skilled Lydians and Ionian Greeks he had imported from his new satrapy in Asia Minor. Then, wasting little time, the Great King turned eastward and marched on the as yet unsubdued peoples who inhabited the Iranian lands north and east of the great Dasht-e-Kavīr salt flats, including the land of Aria. Next, he moved northeastward into the valleys of the Oxus River system, which empties into the Aral Sea about three hundred miles west of the Caspian. The land of Bactria, along the eastern edge of this system, fell before the Persian myriads, as did the region of northwestern India known as Gandara (or Gandaritis) soon afterward.

Through these eastern conquests, by late in 540 Cyrus had nearly doubled the size of his empire. Finally, he felt confident enough to take on the Medes' old ally, Babylonia, and within a few months had reached Mesopotamia's rich alluvial plains. The Babylonian king, Nabonidus, mustered his own army to meet the invaders, but he and his soldiers were no match for the combat-hardened Persian forces. By early October 539, Cyrus's army had taken the city of Opis, on the Tigris River about a hundred miles north of Babylon, and about a week later his general, Gobryas, led the troops to the walls of the capital itself. Because both the powerful Babylonian priests and a majority of the local nobles and common people detested Nabonidus for promoting the moon god, Sin, and other deities over Babylonia's traditional and popular chief god, Marduk, there had already been widespread defections to the Persian side; and Gobryas now entered and took control of the city without a fight, cheered on by many locals, who saw the Persians as

A Persian Army Camp

In the Cyropaedia, *Xenophon provides the following information about how Cyrus arranged his army camps, a system presumably followed by later Persian kings and generals.*

"At the very beginning Cyrus made this rule, that his tent should be pitched facing the east; and then he determined, first, how far from the royal pavilion the spearmen of his guard should have their tent; next he assigned a place on the right for the bakers, on the left for the cooks, on the right for the horses, and on the left for the rest of the pack animals. And everything else was so organized that everyone knew his own place in camp—both its size and its location. . . . For Cyrus considered orderliness to be a good thing to practice in the management of . . . all the departments of an army. . . . Accordingly, he himself took up his position in the middle of the camp in the belief that this situation was the most secure. Then came his most trusty followers . . . and next to them in a circle he had his horsemen and charioteers. . . . Moreover, he had the peltasts [javelin men] and bowmen sleep on their arms [weapons] . . . in order that, if there should be occasion to go into action even at night, they might be ready for it. . . . And all the officers had banners over their tents . . . [so that] the aides under Cyrus were acquainted with the location of the various officers and were familiar with the banner of each one."

Cyrus the Great enters Babylon in triumph in late October 539 B.C. At that time, the famous city on the Euphrates River was so large that the ninety-foot-high defensive wall encircling it was over eleven miles long. One of the city's marvels was a three-hundred-foot-high ziggerat, or tower, with a shrine to the Babylonian god Marduk at its summit.

liberators.[23] Cyrus himself made a triumphant entry into the city on October 29, stating in his first official proclamation: "I am Cyrus, king of the universe, Great King, mighty king, king of Babylon, king of Sumer and Akkad, king of the world quarters."[24]

With the fall of Babylon, Cyrus added Babylonia's imperial possessions, including all of southern Mesopotamia and most of Palestine, to his own empire, which now stretched from the shores of the Aegean Sea in the west to India in the east. That left Egypt as the only one of the former great Near Eastern powers that had not yet fallen under Persian domination. Cyrus planned to bring the Nile civilization into the Persian fold and in the late 530s charged his son, Cambyses, with raising and training a huge new army for that purpose.

But Persia's first great ruler did not live to see this prodigious undertaking come to pass. In about 530, while cam-

paigning in the east near the Aral Sea, he died shortly after suffering a battle wound. His body was carried back to Pasargadae and placed in a simple but beautiful stone tomb, which survives to this day as a monument to one of the most ambitious and talented rulers in history. As Bausani puts it, "His religious tolerance, the moderation with which he treated the defeated . . . and his considerable ability as an army leader explain the universal praise that was accorded Cyrus the Great even by Babylonians and Greeks."[25] Indeed, one such Greek, Xenophon, believed "this man to be deserving of all admiration," and added that "Cyrus was most handsome of person, most generous of heart, most devoted to learning, and most ambitious, so that he endured all sorts of labor and faced all sorts of danger."[26] Rulers like Cyrus, who command such extraordinary respect from subjects and enemies alike, are rare in the historical annals. Persia would not see his like again.

3 Cambyses and Darius: The Empire Expands

The implementation of imperial policies and military reforms Cyrus had begun continued after his death. His immediate successors, Cambyses II and Darius I, further expanded the empire, already the largest in history up to that time; and under Darius, the Achaemenid realm reached its greatest extent. The ambitious and productive Darius also proved himself to be an effective administrator and a great builder of large-scale roads, canals, and palaces befitting a mighty empire. It seems, though, that he did not impress everyone. Herodotus mentions an old Persian saying that "because of his imposition of regular taxes, and other similar measures . . . Darius was a tradesman . . . being out for profit wherever he could get it."[27] Of course, this derisive assessment was filtered through Herodotus's anti-Persian bias; also, it is not truly a Persian viewpoint, for the Persians in Fars did not have to pay taxes. Herodotus probably heard it from resentful members of one of the empire's subject peoples, who *did* have to pay taxes. The remark, along with many later negative descriptions of Darius by Greeks, who were understandably indignant over his invasion of their homeland, does not do justice to his genuine talent, hard work, and many far-reaching accomplishments.

Cambyses in Egypt

Darius's noteworthy deeds were so numerous, in fact, that historically they greatly overshadow those of his predecessor, Cambyses. This is partly because Cambyses, Cyrus's eldest son, had a relatively short reign of eight years and therefore did not have time to achieve all he might have had he ruled for thirty-six years, as Darius did. Yet Cambyses' achievements, though few in number, were by no means trivial. Cyrus had assigned him the task of preparing an invasion of Egypt, and on his father's death Cambyses continued Cyrus's massive military buildup. This included the introduction of Persia's first fleet of ships, a tactical asset for which the Persians had, up to this time, encountered no need. Cambyses correctly reasoned that his army would be unable to live off the land while crossing the barren desert wasteland that formed a barrier between southern Palestine and the fertile Nile delta. But it could easily make the crossing if supported and

A modern artist's depiction of the Persian king Cambyses killing the sacred Egyptian Bull of Apis. This story was likely fabricated later in an attempt to blacken his name and memory, for evidence suggests that the animal died while he was campaigning in Ethiopia.

supplied by ships sailing along the nearby coast.[28] Persia's transformation at this time from solely a land power to master of both sea and land widened the scope of its potential future conquests, making possible, for example, the later invasions of Europe by Cambyses' successors.

In 526 B.C., shortly before launching the Egyptian invasion, Cambyses committed an act that, along with other disreputable deeds attributed to him, earned him a reputation for cruelty and violence. His younger brother Bardiya, whom the Greeks called Smerdis, had been Cyrus's favorite and was much more popular than Cambyses among both nobles and commoners. Before dying, Cyrus made it clear that Bardiya was to inherit the empire's eastern satrapies, while Cambyses should get the western ones. Evidently, Cambyses worried that after he departed for Egypt his brother might lead a rebellion and usurp the western portion of the realm. So a secret assassination plan was conceived and carried out. As Herodotus tells it:

Cambyses dreamt that a messenger came to him from Persia with the news that Smerdis was sitting on the royal throne and that his head touched the sky. In alarm lest the dream should mean that his brother would kill him and reign in his stead, Cambyses sent Prexaspes, the most trusted of his Persian friends, to make away with [kill] him. Prexaspes went up-country to Susa and did the deed—according to one account he took his victim out hunting, according to another he lured him down to the Persian Gulf and drowned him.[29]

Confident that he had eliminated his only potential rival, early in 525 Cambyses entered Egypt at the head of a huge army. Unfortunately for the Egyptians, their pharaoh, Amasis, who was a capable war leader, had just died, leaving his inexperienced young son Psamtik III (or Psammetichos) to face the Persian threat. The armies met near Pelusium, on the seacoast just east of the Nile delta. The well-trained Persians crushed their opponents, causing the young pharaoh to flee for his life; and in fact, so decisive was Cambyses' victory that the country fell into his grasp without any further pitched battles. In this way, he brought the last of the former great Near Eastern empires into Persia's grasp.

Cambyses remained in Egypt for the next three years or so and the exact nature of his deeds during this interval is unclear. Lurid stories abound in the works of Herodotus and other ancient writers about how the Persian monarch committed cruel and sacrilegious acts and unnecessarily caused the deaths of thousands of his own soldiers. For instance, Cambyses supposedly savagely abused and burned Amasis's mummified corpse, publicly mutilated a sacred Egyptian bull, and attempted to invade Nubia, a land south of Egypt, without bringing sufficient provisions for his men, many of whom starved to death or turned to cannibalism.

Modern scholars have dismissed these charges as greatly exaggerated if not outright fabrications. For example, while it has been confirmed that Cambyses

Why the Persians Had Thin Skulls

When Herodotus visited Egypt in the late 450s B.C., his guides showed him the site of the great battle of Pelusium in which Cambyses had defeated the Egyptian army three-quarters of a century before. In his Histories, *the historian included this bizarre but fascinating observation.*

"At the place where this battle was fought I saw a very odd thing, which the natives had told me about. The bones still lay there, those of the Persian dead separate from those of the Egyptian . . . and I noticed that the skulls of the Persians are so thin that the merest touch with a pebble will pierce them, but those of the Egyptians, on the other hand, are so tough that it is hardly possible to break them with a blow from a stone. I was told . . . that the reason was that the Egyptians shave their heads from childhood, so that the bone of the skull is indurated [hardened] by the action of the sun . . . and the thinness of the Persians' skulls rests upon a similar principle: namely that they have always worn felt skullcaps, to guard their heads from the sun."

campaigned in northern Nubia, his reasons for cutting short the expedition remain unknown; and the charges of his thoughtless lack of preparation seem absurd considering his recent careful preparations for invading Egypt. By contrast, there is strong evidence that Cambyses did order the execution of young Psamtik and also damaged and looted some Egyptian temples; however, though at odds with Cyrus's kindlier treatment of beaten enemies, such acts were fairly commonplace for victorious conquerors in ancient times. It is certainly plausible that the scandalous stories about Cambyses that Herodotus heard when visiting Egypt many decades later were colored by the natives' hatred for the man who had reduced their country to servile status.

Reign of the Impostor

Whatever Cambyses actually did during his stay in Egypt, early in 522 he decided to return to the Persian homeland. He had only just begun his long journey when he received news that a man named Gautama had instigated a rebellion and stolen the throne in Ecbatana. Gautama (whom the Greeks called "the False Smerdis") claimed to be Cambyses' brother Bardiya, to whom the impostor bore an uncanny physical resemblance; and because the murder of the real Bardiya was a secret, many Persians and their subject peoples had no reason to suspect that Gautama was not in fact whom he claimed to be. A portion of the famous inscription later carved by Darius on the face of a cliff in Behistun (or Bisitun), southwest of Ecbatana, reads:

> After Cambyses went to Egypt . . . there was great deceit in the land,

both in Persia and Media and in the other provinces. . . . There arose a Magian [Median priest], by name Gautama. . . . On the fourteenth day of the month Viyakhna [March 11, 522 B.C.] he rose up. He deceived the people, saying, "I am Bardiya, son of Cyrus, brother of Cambyses." Then all the people became estranged from Cambyses and went over to him [Gautama]. . . . He seized the kingdom.[30]

The events of the following weeks and months remain sketchy and unclear, possibly because of a later deliberate cover-up for political reasons. Shortly after hearing about Gautama's rebellion, Cambyses died under mysterious circumstances. Some accounts say the cause was the onset of gangrene after an accidental knife wound; others claim that Cambyses was mentally unbalanced and, in a fit of despair over the bad news from Ecbatana, took his own life. With the king dead, Gautama held the throne for about seven months (March to September 522). Then a small group of powerful Persian nobles conspired to kill him. Having done the deed, they placed one of their own number on the throne—Darius, who belonged to a branch of the Achaemenid family (not the one that had produced Cyrus and Cambyses) and therefore did have a legitimate claim. Darius later boasted in the Behistun carving:

> On the tenth day of the month Bagayadi [September 29], I slew that Gautama the Magian and his chief associates, [at] a stronghold . . . [in] the land of Nisaya in Media; I deprived him of the kingdom; by the will of Ahura-Mazda [the chief Persian god], I became king.[31]

The Cliff Carving at Behistun

In this excerpt from his great History of the Persian Empire, *A. T. Olmstead describes how Darius appears in the monumental (ten-by-eighteen-foot) panel he ordered carved into the side of a cliff some five hundred feet above the ground in Behistun.*

"Darius, a fine Aryan type with high brow and straight nose, stands his natural height, five feet ten inches. On his head is the war crown, and . . . gold band studded with oval jewels and rosettes. His front hair is carefully frizzed, and his drooping mustache is neatly twirled at the tip. . . . The square beard is arranged in four rows of curls alternating with straight strands, quite in the manner of those of his Assyrian predecessors. A long robe covers the whole of his stocky body . . . and, below, it is draped at the side to allow a glimpse of the trousers and beneath them the laced shoes. The king's left hand grasps the strung bow tipped with a duck's head; his right hand is uplifted in worship of [the god] Ahura-Mazda. . . . Under the king's left foot, flat on his back and one foot lifted in agony, lies the robed Gautama, stretching out his hands in vain supplication. Before their conqueror stand the other rebels, their necks roped together, their hands tied behind their backs."

An artist's sketch of a section of the famous Behistun carving showing Darius I triumphing over his enemies, including the usurper Gautama (lying beneath the king's foot).

Why did Darius and his colleagues remove the royal pretender? Darius himself later claimed that Gautama ruled harshly and murdered many innocent people, and that "the people feared him for his tyranny."[32] On the other hand, considerable evidence suggests that Gautama may have been a zealous religious and social reformer whose attempts to institute too much change too quickly alarmed the more conservative nobles, who preferred to maintain the status quo. Either way, they would have felt justified in eliminating him.

One very intriguing possibility is that the man the nobles killed was not a pretender at all, but in fact the real Bardiya. According to this scenario, Cambyses did not kill Bardiya, who, backed by Darius and the other nobles, seized the throne while Cambyses lingered in Egypt. Once in power, Bardiya revealed himself to be a reformer; and when he pushed his agenda too fast, those nobles who had at first backed him balked and decided to eliminate him. They then attempted to justify their act by claiming he was a rank impostor and that they had therefore saved the empire from a treacherous ruse. If this is in fact what happened, it explains why Darius's later claims that the usurper committed tyrannical acts do not square with Bardiya's reputation for kindness and civility. It also sheds light on the mystery of Cambyses' death shortly after the usurper took power. The king may have been murdered by his own officers, who preferred Bardiya over him; in that case, the other accounts of his death would have been fabrications concocted later to support the cover story that an impostor had seized the throne. The real truth will probably never be known. What is certain is that Darius became king late in 522, launching a reign that would carry the Persian Empire to new heights.

Reunifying and Reorganizing the Empire

Before he could put his plans for the empire into effect, however, Darius had first to keep the realm from falling apart. As soon as the news spread that Bardiya (or whoever) had been killed, many of the satrapies, attempting to take advantage of a central government apparently in disarray, revolted. Scholar Percy Sykes states in his *History of Persia*:

> The governors of the distant provinces, thinking possibly that the empire of Persia would share the fate of Media, desired to carve out kingdoms for themselves. Darius, therefore, had to conquer, and in some cases to reconquer, the many kingdoms of which the empire consisted; and there were times when only his army and a few of the provinces remained true to him. The provinces of Elam and Babylonia were the first to break into open revolt. . . . Meanwhile, Media, taking advantage of the embarrassments of the new monarch, tried to recover her old position under the leadership of a certain Phraortes, who claimed to be a descendant of Cyaxares. . . . As if this were not enough, even Persia [that is, the Persian homeland of Fars, or Persis] revolted and followed a second impostor, Vahyazdata by name, claiming to be Bardiya.[33]

nation, in the span of little more than a year he methodically crushed the revolts one by one. Once firmly in control of his reunited empire, he served a grim warning to any future would-be rebels by making a gruesome example of the Median upstart Phraortes. The unfortunate man suffered the loss of his nose, ears, tongue, and eyes, after which he was impaled and hung, still living, for all to see on Ecbatana's royal gate. Another way that Darius demonstrated he was a king to be reckoned with was by memorializing his victory in stone: The carving at Behistun, begun in the months that followed, showed the king standing triumphant before nine subservient rebel leaders, all bound at their necks by a single rope.

Darius's next task was to reorganize the empire he had saved from oblivion. He divided the realm into twenty satrapies, retaining Cyrus's idea of making the satraps' secretaries report directly to the king. But Darius, who had learned a hard lesson about what these governors might do if given too much power, allowed them no military authority at all. "In fact," Bausani explains,

> the military forces of each satrapy were under the orders of a commander completely independent of the satrap and directly responsible to the king himself. This ingenious arrangement enabled a mutual check to be kept on the civil and military authorities, both of which were directly responsible to the sovereign, who then employed his "eyes and ears" in the guise of special inspectors, to visit the satrapies and see that no rebellions or separatist movements arose. Another ingenious feature was the fact that

Darius I, who came to power in 522 or 521 B.C., stands shaded by servants while the great god Ahura-Mazda floats above.

If, as is likely, the rebels believed that Darius was a weak and ineffectual leader who would be powerless against them, they were dead wrong. In a brilliant display of tactical ability and sheer determi-

In this stone panel found in the ruins of the palace at Persepolis, Median officials pay homage to Darius (seated on throne at right), who reorganized the empire's provinces and tax system.

there were not as many military commanders as satraps, since each of the former commanded the military forces of four or five satrapies.[34]

Darius also instituted a new form of taxation in the satrapies. Before his reforms, the provinces periodically had been expected to give the king "gifts" of gold and other valuables; but no specific amounts had been fixed and satraps had often offered whatever they claimed they could afford. Darius assigned standard annual tax rates to each province and ordered the richest provinces, Egypt and Babylonia, to pay more than the others, a system that ensured a more reliable flow of wealth into his central treasury.[35]

Darius's standardization of the tax system was greatly facilitated by his introduction of coinage, an idea borrowed from the Lydians (before this, Persian currency consisted of bars of gold and other metals, as well as goods such as grain, cattle, and slaves). His gold coins were called darics, either in homage to his own name or after

zarik, the Persian word for "golden." Use of this formal, standardized money also stimulated increases in trade, both among satrapies and with foreign nations.

An Innovative and Effective Ruler

During his reign, Darius instituted other projects and measures that were designed, like his new coinage, to strengthen the new organization he had imposed on his far-flung empire. These efforts further showcased his talents as a highly innovative, constructive, and effective administrator. For example, he correctly reasoned that one way to bind his distant provinces more securely to the central authority was to improve long-distance communications. This meant building well-maintained and well-guarded roads over which both his couriers and armies could move more quickly. Such roads would also better facili-

Remnants of the Palace at Susa

From his book
Ancient Persia,
*scholar John Curtis
here describes some
of the large-scale
and ornate
construction Darius
carried out at Susa.*

"It is a mark of Susa's importance that Darius undertook much building work here; extensive traces have been found in excavations of the site. Most impressive are the Apadana, or audience hall, and an adjoining palace consisting of rooms grouped around large courtyards in the Babylonian tradition. . . . The plan of the Apadana . . . consists of a square columned hall with towers at the four corners of the building and, on three sides, porticoes between the towers. The stone columns were very elaborate and supported capitals in the form of two bulls back to back. . . . In the palace that Darius constructed adjoining the Apadana were panels of polychrome glazed bricks, probably decorating courtyard walls. One shows a pair of winged, human-headed lions beneath a winged disk, and another a frieze of royal guards, the so-called 'Immortals.'"

A grand staircase leading to the east side of the Apadana (a large audience hall supported by tall pillars and flanked by square guard towers) at the palace at Persepolis.

tate the movement of trade goods from one province to another. The most famous of the so-called "royal roads" Darius built stretched over 1,500 miles from Susa to Sardis. Herodotus, who actually traveled on this road, describes it this way:

This modern photo shows the ruins of a gatehouse at Persepolis, its entrance flanked by Assyrian-type bulls with human heads.

At intervals all along the road are recognized stations, with excellent inns, and the road itself is safe to travel by, as it never leaves inhabited country. In Lydia and Phrygia [in Asia Minor], over a distance of . . . about 330 miles—there are 20 stations. . . . The total number of stations, or posthouses, on the road from Sardis to Susa is 111. . . . Traveling at the rate of 150 furlongs [18 miles] a day, a man will take just ninety days to make the journey.[36]

Darius established royal couriers, horsemen who frequently changed mounts at each road station, "slept in the saddle" (like the Pony Express riders in the American West), and covered the distance in just fifteen days. A similar royal road stretched from Ecbatana northeastward into distant Bactria.

Other large-scale projects initiated under Darius included impressive canals and palaces. Some twenty-five hundred years before the construction of the Suez Canal, he completed an artificial channel (already begun by the Egyptians) that ran some 125 miles from the Nile to the Red Sea, thus linking the Mediterranean with the Indian Ocean (and, by way of the Gulf of Oman, with the Persian Gulf). He also erected spacious new royal buildings at Susa and began work on a magnificent palace complex at Persepolis (to the southwest of Pasargadae in Fars), which his successors would complete.

Darius also devoted his attention to military development and new conquests. Until his time the vast majority of troops in the Persian army were native conscripts from Fars or the various provinces. His most important military reform was a major increase in the use of paid foreign mercenaries to supplement the regular soldiers, a move made possible by the huge influx of wealth he enjoyed from expanded taxation and trade.

To keep his large standing army busy, as well as to expand his power and influence, in 519 the Great King led an expedition against the Saka, a people who inhabited the remote, rugged region northwest of India. Quickly conquered, the area became the empire's newest satrapy. But Darius's eastern campaigns were destined to be largely forgotten, for soon afterward he turned westward to attempt the subjugation of the Scythians (or Scyths), the semicivilized inhabitants of the region west of the Black Sea. This new expedition would prove fateful for Darius and also for his successors, for it would mark Persia's first foray into Europe, a continental fortress at whose southern gates the tiny but tenacious Greek city-states stood guard.

4 Of Sovereigns, Serfs, and Slaves: Life in the Persian Heartland

Under Darius I, the Persian Empire reached the heights of political and military development it would maintain, with minor variations, until its fall in the fourth century B.C. The social and religious customs of his time also remained substantially unchanged in the generations that followed, so that everyday life during his reign was fairly representative of Persian culture in general. The problem modern

scholars frequently face is deciding which elements of that culture were distinctly Persian and which were Median, Babylonian, Assyrian, Lydian, and so forth. The Persian Empire was, after all, composed of many diverse lands and peoples, with their own languages, customs, and religions. Although the Persian kings almost exclusively appointed native Persian nobles to high posts in the satrapies and the

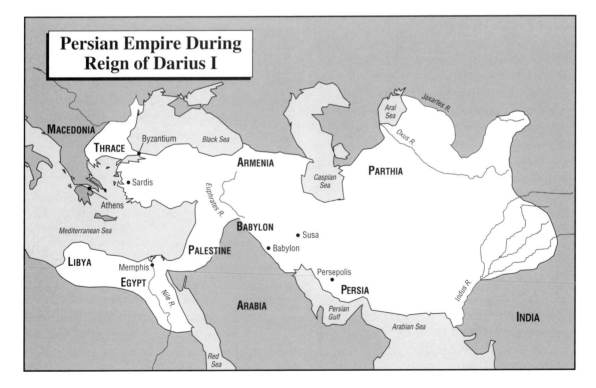

Persian Empire During Reign of Darius I

army and through these individuals controlled the empire, generally the ruling elite allowed the non-Persian residents of the provinces to retain their local ways. Thus, there were really two Persias—the larger empire, composed mainly of non-Persian cultures, and the much smaller Persian heartland centered in western Iran. Under Darius and his successors, this heartland encompassed not only Fars, with its grand palace sites of Pasargadae and Persepolis, but also the uplands surrounding Ecbatana and the fertile plains around Susa.

Archaeological evidence from this heartland reveals a society that was largely a fusion of the cultures of various earlier Mesopotamian and Iranian peoples. This is because the Persians, like the later Romans, readily borrowed ideas and customs from others. Herodotus writes, "No race is so ready to adopt foreign ways as the Persian; for instance, they wear the Median costume because they think it handsomer than their own, and their soldiers wear the Egyptian corselet."[37] Other examples included the upland Persians' horse-breeding and sheep-herding practices, in imitation of earlier Iranian nomads; the lowland Persians' tilling of the soil in the age-old Babylonian manner; and the Persian adoption of Assyrian military and political ideas.

Unfortunately, narrowing the focus to Persia's heartland does not fully illuminate Persian society. The majority of surviving Persian records contain little information about cultural pursuits and everyday life and those that do provide such data mainly concentrate on the members of the royal court and upper classes. Greek sources such as Herodotus and Xenophon are more helpful, but like

Three well-to-do ancient Persians in their typical flamboyant garb. A nobleman is flanked by two warriors wearing felt tiaras on their heads.

most other ancient historians they tended to dwell on the deeds and customs of the well-to-do and powerful and only rarely described the lives of common people. As Alessandro Bausani reminds us:

> When considering the ancient history of Asia . . . one should always bear in mind that expressions such as "the Persian people," "the Medes," or "the Babylonians" are only conventions which really mean "the few thousand people forming the ruling class of the states termed Persian, Median, Babylonian, etc." Of these few thousand people, and only these, we are familiar with the religion, language, art, philosophy, and aspirations.[38]

Indeed, so little substantive information exists about the common people who made up the bulk of Persia's population that it is uncertain whether, for instance, they worshiped the same gods the king did or treated women in the same manner as the wealthy and highborn.

The Social Ladder

Because information about the lifestyles of Persia's rich and famous is more complete and reliable, it seems fitting to examine the upper classes first, beginning with the king and his court. Darius and Persia's other so-called Great Kings were absolute monarchs thought to be the empire's ulti-mate sources of law, dignity, and honor. The only limit to a king's power was that he was expected to observe Persia's customs and to consult his top-ranking nobles before making decisions of great importance. Not surprisingly, fearful of incurring his disfavor, these advisers only rarely disagreed with him.

In court and in public, the king wore a flowing robe of Median design, dyed purple, the traditional hue of royalty in ancient times, and interwoven with golden threads. On his head rested a magnificent crown encrusted with brilliant gems; he also regularly wore beautifully crafted earrings, chains, and bracelets and sat on an elaborately decorated throne. On greeting or approaching the Great King, all of his subjects, including the highest nobles,

A Degrading and Blasphemous Act?

Most Greeks who witnessed pros-kenysis, *the act of prostration performed by Persians before their king, found it degrading and also blasphemous. In this excerpt from his* Anabasis, *the Greek historian Arrian recounts how Callisthenes, one of Alexander the Great's officers, felt about such prostration.*

"Do not forget that there is a difference between honoring a man and worshipping a god. The distinction between the two has been marked in many ways: for instance, by the building of temples, the erection of statues; the dedication of sacred ground—all these are for the gods. . . . Yet of all these things not one is so important as this very custom of prostration. Men greet each other with a kiss; but a god, far above us on his mysterious throne, it is not lawful for us to touch—and that is why we proffer him the homage of bowing to the earth before him. . . . It is wrong, therefore, to ignore these distinctions; we ought not to make a man look bigger than he is by paying him excessive and extravagant honor, or, at the same time, impiously to degrade the gods . . . by putting them in this matter on the same level as men."

were expected to prostrate themselves, facedown on the floor or ground, before him, an act the Greeks called *proskenysis*. The following description by Xenophon of one of Cyrus's grand processions illustrates the lavish pomp surrounding the Persian monarch and his court.

> When the palace gates were thrown open, there were led out at the head of the procession four abreast some exceptionally handsome bulls. . . . Next after the bulls came horses, a sacrifice for the Sun; and after them came a chariot. . . . It was drawn by white horses with a yoke of gold and wreathed with garlands. . . . After that came a . . . chariot with horses covered with purple trappings, and behind it followed men carrying fire on a great altar. Next after these Cyrus himself upon a chariot appeared . . . wearing his tiara upright, a purple tunic . . . (no one but the king may wear such a one), trousers of scarlet dye about his legs, and a mantle all of purple. . . . And when [the spectators] saw him, they all prostrated themselves before him. . . . When Cyrus's chariot had come forth, four thousand lancers took the lead . . . and his mace-bearers, about three hundred in number, followed next in gala attire. . . . Next came Cyrus's private stud of horses, about two hundred in all, led along with gold-mounted bridles and covered over with embroidered housings.[39]

Directly below the Great King on the Persian social ladder were the chief nobles, who were in effect feudal lords not unlike those of later medieval Europe. Although in theory all of Persia's lands belonged to the king, Darius and his succes-

sors regularly granted estates and other landholdings to the nobles who served as officers and cavalrymen in the army. Appropriately, holdings of various sizes were designated by military terms; there were, for example, "bow lands," "horse lands," "chariot lands," and so forth. The owner of each kind of parcel was obligated to provide men and equipment for the army. Thus, the lord of a bow land, consisting of about fifty-two acres, was expected to supply one archer. These were among the smallest estates; some of the king's favorites lorded over parcels of many thousands of acres.

Persian court dignitaries strike a formal pose (right hands folded over left) in this portion of a staircase relief from the palace at Persepolis.

Maintaining these estates and the large houses of their owners required many kinds of workers, ranging from farmers and field hands to horse trainers and smiths to cooks and chambermaids. A few of these were paid freemen, but most were unpaid serfs and slaves. Like their medieval counterparts, serfs under the Achaemenid rulers were allotted small farming plots on which they lived and worked in exchange for their promise to supply the owner with a hefty share of the harvest. On these plots, the serfs built ramshackle huts, usually of mud-brick, stone, or thatch. While some serfs did rise to positions of responsibility and importance within the self-contained worlds of their owners' estates, most were perpetually in debt to those owners and therefore unable to escape their subservient condition.

As in all ancient societies, slaves occupied the bottom of the social ladder, although ironically in Persia a slave had perhaps a slightly better chance of earning his or her freedom than a serf did. Olmstead comments:

> Free men might be enslaved for debt or as a punishment for a crime. Parents might sell their children in times of stress. Foreign names [on surviving tablets and monuments] betray the captive taken in war or the slave brought from abroad. Most slaves, however, were born in the home, since marriage of slaves for breeding purposes was profitable. Unless he ran away from his master or falsely claimed free birth, the slave was, as a rule, well treated. Often he was entrusted with responsible duties, and on rare occasions he was freed.[40]

Between the rich upper class and the unpaid lower classes ranged the paid freemen, most of whom were unskilled laborers. Besides those who toiled on estates, some worked on large-scale building projects like canals and royal palaces while others served long stretches in the army. The few skilled freemen—among them bakers, butchers, carpenters, and artisans—composed a small lower-middle class. Higher on the social ladder were merchants, who often made comfortable livings trading such commodities as purple dyes and textiles from Phoenicia (on the coast of Palestine); perfumes from Arabia, timber from the Greek island of Crete; grain and glass from Egypt; and spices and gold dust from India.

The Persian Gender Gap

Not much is known about the customs and attitudes of the members of these various social classes, largely because of the scarcity of surviving Persian documents. What is known derives mainly from Greek sources and primarily pertains to the upper classes. Herodotus, for example, tells us that the Persian nobility was both arrogant and self-absorbed. "Themselves they consider in every way superior to everyone else in the world, and allow other nations a share of good qualities decreasing according to distance, the furthest off [from the Persian heartland] being the worst."[41]

Herodotus also dwells at some length on the importance of "manliness" to the Persians, for Persia was no less male dominated than other ancient societies. "After prowess in fighting," he writes, "the chief proof of manliness is to be the father of a

Fashion Styles of Persia's Rich and Famous

This brief excerpt from Xenophon's Cyropaedia *reveals that upper-class Persian men attempted to enhance their appearance through the use of stylish fashions, shoe lifts, and makeup.*

"[Cyrus the Great] chose to wear the Median dress himself and persuaded his associates also to adopt it; for he thought that if anyone had any personal defect, that dress would help to conceal it, and that it made the wearer look very tall and very handsome. For they have shoes of such a form that without being detected the wearer can easily put something into the soles so as to make him look taller than he is. He encouraged also the fashion of penciling the eyes, that they might seem more lustrous than they are, and of using cosmetics to make the complexion look better than nature made it."

---

large family of boys. Those who have [the] most sons receive an annual present from the king." About the upbringing of upper-class boys, he adds:

> The period of a boy's education is between the ages of five and twenty, and they are taught three things only: to ride, to use the bow, and to speak the truth. Before the age of five a boy lives with the [household] women and never sees his father, the object being to spare the father distress if the child should die in the early stages of its upbringing.[42]

By contrast, women apparently received little or no education and in general were treated as inferiors. This can be inferred partly from the prevalence of polygamy; many upper-class men had several wives and, according to Herodotus, a number of concubines, or live-in mistresses, as well. For the most part, women led secluded lives, as did many Greek women, who spent much of their time in the household's "women's quarters"; an important difference was that Greek women kept busy at spinning and other domestic tasks, while upper-class Persian ladies were raised to think that any kind of work was degrading and should therefore be performed only by their servants.

Despite the social gap between the genders, Persian men and women at least sometimes felt and expressed genuine romantic love, as evidenced by the famous story of Abradatas and Panthea from Xenophon's *Cyropaedia*. The poignancy of their parting as he leaves for battle has rarely been surpassed in later literature:

> Panthea bade all who stood near to retire and then she said: "Abradatas, if ever a woman loved her husband more than her own life, I think you know that I, too, am such a one. . . . With the affection that you know I have for you, I swear to you by my love

for you and yours for me that, of a truth, I would far rather go down into the earth with you, if you approve yourself a gallant soldier, than live disgraced with one disgraced, so worthy of the noblest lot have I deemed both you and myself." . . . Abradatas, touched by her words, laid his hand upon her head, and lifting up his eyes toward heaven prayed, saying: "Grant me . . . that I may show myself a husband worthy of Panthea." . . . And then at once his chariot rolled away, but she followed after, unknown to him, until Abradatas turned round and saw her and said, "Have a brave heart, Panthea, and farewell!"[43]

A Man Who Owes Money Is Bound to Tell Lies

Panthea's mention of being "worthy of the noblest lot" was undoubtedly a reference to the lofty and strict (but probably unwritten) code of honor and honesty aspired to by the Persian upper classes. Many of the precepts of this code were emphasized by Darius I, who set himself up as a model for others to follow, both in life and in the inscription he ordered carved on his tomb:

> To that which is just I am a friend, to that which is unjust I am no friend. I do not wish that the weak should suffer harm at the hands of the powerful, nor that the powerful should suffer harm at the hands of the weak. . . . The follower after falsehood do I detest. . . . Who works for me I reward according to his work. Who does ill I punish according to the ill he has done. . . . If one man speaks ill of another, I do not give him credence until he has provided proof. If a man acts to the best of his ability, I am satisfied.[44]

The hatred of falsehood Darius expressed was especially significant. According to Herodotus, the Persians "consider telling lies more disgraceful than anything else,

Upper-class Persian women led comfortable but largely secluded lives, as illustrated in this modern depiction of a lady of means entertaining a female friend as a servant looks on.

and, next to that, owing money. There are many reasons for their horror of debt, but the chief is their conviction that a man who owes money is bound also to tell lies."[45] Their penalty for lying is unknown but punishments for crimes of any sort were generally severe, for upper and lower classes alike. Murder, rape, and treason, for example, incurred the death penalty, variously carried out by live burial, crucifixion, or suffocation in a pit of ashes. Even comparatively minor offenses might result in blinding or the mutilation of hands and feet.

On the lighter side, the majority of Persians who followed society's rules were, Herodotus and other ancient writers agree, a congenial folk. Equals customarily greeted one another with a kiss on the mouth and near-equals with a peck on the cheek, fairly common practice in Western societies today. They were also fond of feasting and drinking wine, particularly when celebrating birthdays. "A rich Persian on his birthday," Herodotus explains,

will have an ox or a horse or a camel or a donkey baked whole in the oven and served up at table, and the poor some smaller beast. The main dishes at their meals are few, but they have many sorts of dessert, the various courses being served separately. It is this custom that has made them say that the Greeks leave the table hungry, because we never have anything worth mentioning after the first course.[46]

An Eternal Struggle Between Light and Darkness

Other celebrations must have been connected to religious observances. Most of Persia's subject peoples continued worshiping their own native gods even after their lands had been absorbed into the imperial framework. The Iranians themselves were at first strictly polytheistic, praying to several nature gods of Aryan

Upper-class Persian men enjoying a meal. Very little is known about what they ate, outside of the passing remarks by Herodotus (in his famous history) that they had few main dishes but many desserts.

In this drawing of a stone relief from Persepolis, a Persian king worships Ahura-Mazda while people from different parts of the ruler's empire stand below and support him.

origin known as *daevas*. Among these was a sky god, Ahura-Mazda, already worshiped in the northern reaches of the Iranian plateau by the late second millennium B.C.

Eventually a great prophet arose—Zarathustra, whom the Greeks and other Westerners came to call Zoroaster. The exact time of Zoroaster's life and preaching remains uncertain and controversial; most scholars place him either in the early ninth or early sixth centuries B.C. Essentially, he was a monotheist, singling out Ahura-Mazda, the "wise lord," as the one true god. Ahura-Mazda was supposedly engaged in an eternal struggle with an evil force or devil, at first known as Angra-Mainu and later as Ahriman. Later Persians often pictured Ahura-Mazda as he appears in the Behistun carving of Darius, an ardent proponent of Zoroaster's beliefs. As described by Olmstead, the carved image of the god floats above the king's head.

On his head the bearded god wears the cylindrical hat, flaring at the top and distinguished from the king's by the horns of divinity and an eight-rayed solar disk. . . . His garment is the draped robe, whose full sleeve curves down to the braceleted wrists. His left hand grasps the ring which bestows sovereignty on monarchs; his right hand, palm open, is raised in blessing. He is lifted aloft on a huge ring [equipped with] wings. . . . From the ring stretch down objects which have been described as two-forked lightning bolts.[47]

Zoroastrianism, the religion derived from the prophet's teachings, and to which Darius and his successors subscribed, developed a number of central tenets. One of these was the concept that an ethical person is one who diligently tends to personal concerns while coexisting in peace and harmony with his or her neighbors.[48] Another tenet of the religion

held that the devout must constantly resist being seduced by the old *daevas*, who were actually evil spirits or demons in league with Ahriman. Thus, the faith pictured human life as a struggle similar to that in which the god itself was engaged—a battle between the forces of good and evil, between light and darkness.

These and other Zoroastrian ideas and beliefs were, over time, written down in a group of scriptures known collectively as the *Avesta*. A priesthood also developed. Originally of Median origin, the priests were called Magi; that the modern words "magic" and "magician" developed from their name is no accident, for they introduced into the faith diverse rituals based on dreams, astrology, and magic.[49] The Magi also zealously promoted the idea

Hymns of Praise for Ahura-Mazda

In this section of Zoroaster's last recorded prayer from the Avesta *(James Darmesteter's translation as it appears in Olmstead's* History of the Persian Empire*) the prophet is nearing his life's end.*

"I who with Good Thought have set my heart to watch the soul, who have known rewards from Ahura-Mazda for my deeds, while I have power and strength [left in my body] will I teach men to seek after Righteousness. When shall I, as one who knows, see you, Righteousness, and Good Thought, the throne of mightiest Ahura and the Obedience of Mazda? Through this holy word on our tongue may we turn the robber horde to the Greatest [convert the wicked to belief in the one true god]. . . . We strive to offer hymns of praise to you, since you are best able to advance desire for the Beneficent Kingdom [Heaven]. . . . Therefore would I preserve Righteousness and Good Thought forevermore; do you teach me, Ahura-Mazda, by your mouth through your Spirit to proclaim how the First Life shall be."

An ancient Persian Magian and his assistants examine some papyrus scrolls. The elite and mysterious Magi likely made up the strictest, most orthodox level of the state-accepted religion.

that some animals, such as dogs and cattle, were good, while many others were the "creatures of the evil one," which must be destroyed whenever possible. These evil creatures prominently included "creeping things" such as ants, flies, earthworms, frogs, snakes, and so forth.

The Magi also practiced the burial custom of leaving corpses outside to be picked at by birds and other beasts. By contrast, most other Persians did not expose their dead to scavengers. The most common practice was dipping the body in wax and burying it; and even some of the most devout, like Darius, opted to be interred in stone tombs rather than to

follow the Magian custom. This and other discrepancies between the rituals and practices of the Magi and those of other Persians suggest that there may have been different levels or versions of the religion for different groups. Thus, the Magi may have practiced an orthodox version, the king and nobles a less strict one, and the lower classes a still more modified one that allowed some incorporation of the traditional gods. Future archaeological discoveries may shed light on this mystery; for the moment, however, like so many other aspects of Persian life and culture, it remains half shrouded in the mists of time.

5 A Stepping-Stone to Europe: Darius Versus the Greeks

In 512 B.C., Darius led an army through northern Asia Minor, crossed what is now the Bosporus strait, and entered Thrace, the rugged, sparsely inhabited Greek region lying along the northern rim of the Aegean Sea. Most of the Thracian tribes immediately submitted without a fight, after which the expedition moved northward, crossed the Danube River, and entered the vast steppes that later became southern Russia. Historians have long speculated about Darius's motives in initiating this first of Persia's invasions of Europe. Some believe that he was attempting to punish the inhabitants of the steppes, the nomadic Scythians, for a series of devastating raids they had launched into the Near East about a century before. Some feel that he was lured by rumors of vast caches of Scythian gold. And others suggest that the Great King was merely taking the next logical step in the tradition of empire building begun by his predecessors.

Darius was no doubt moved by all of these considerations, but the last, imperial expansion, was likely his strongest motive. And, in fact, persuasive evidence suggests that he had designs on all of Europe. Shortly before his foray into Thrace and Scythia (or perhaps immediately following it), he sent out ships manned by scouts who first cruised and mapped the Greek coasts and then pushed on to southern Italy. They apparently made it no farther west, so Darius never gained an accurate picture of the large size of the Mediterranean-European world and the nature of its lands and peoples; nevertheless, what he already knew about the eastern edges of that world suggested that it was rich in natural resources and ripe for the taking.

Because of its strategic location, just across the Aegean waters from Asia Minor, Persia's westernmost territory, Greece represented an important stepping-stone for Persian penetration of Europe. As it turned out, the Greeks, both in Ionia and mainland Greece, gave Darius much more trouble than he had bargained for. In the two decades following his Scythian expedition, he received the surprising and unwelcome news of Greeks rebelling against him, burning an important Persian city, and even decisively defeating one of his armies. But it is important to realize that, despite the huge significance of these events to the tiny Greek states, the Great King, with immense human and material resources at his disposal, considered them no more than minor setbacks. At no time during the so-called Greek and Persian Wars of the early fifth century B.C.

did Greece pose a serious threat to the overall power and stability of the mighty Persian Empire.

Darius's Scythian Campaign

Darius prepared for his first venture into Europe with some wise preliminary measures. He ordered military officials in his satrapy of Katpatuka (which the Greeks called Cappadocia), bordering the Black Sea in northern Asia Minor, to sail to the northern coast of the sea and raid the nearest villages. This expedition, designed to secure prisoners, was a complete success. Among the captives was the brother of a local chief, who provided the Persians with much valuable information about the Scythians and their lands.

The Scythians were a seminomadic tribal people who made their living mainly by raising cattle and other livestock. Though they had no cities, writing system, or formal government comparable to those of the Persians and Greeks, they were by no means primitive. The Scythian tribes were linked in a loose political federation and the local craftspeople produced fine embroidered textiles; exquisitely decorated leathers; and numerous copper, bronze, and gold artifacts. Scythian warriors were expert horsemen-archers known for their tenacity and also for their custom of collecting as trophies the heads of their defeated enemies; typically, they fashioned the skulls into drinking cups that hung from their belts when not in use.[50]

Though fierce and capable, the Scythians were also wise enough to realize that it would be foolhardy to engage a large,

well-organized army like Darius's in open combat. A traditionally mobile people, they easily fell back, forcing the Persians to waste much time and effort pursuing them. During this strategic retreat, Scythian horsemen constantly harassed Persian foraging parties; the natives also adopted a scorched earth policy, as Herodotus put it, "blocking up all the

The details of this Scythian warrior's costume probably date from a period well after Darius's invasion of Europe.

wells and springs which they passed and trampling the pasture,"[51] so as to deprive the invaders of the use of these resources.

As a soldier trained in a formal and very proud imperial military tradition, Darius found the enemy's tactics cowardly and irritating, and he quickly grew frustrated. He sent a messenger to the chief of the Scythian forces with these words:

> Why on earth, my good sir, do you keep running away? You have, surely, a choice of two alternatives: if you think yourself strong enough to oppose me, stand up and fight, instead of wandering all over the world in your efforts to escape me; or, if you admit that you are too weak, what is the good, even so, of running away? You should rather send earth and water [the sign of submission] to your master . . . and come to a conference.

Idanthyrsus, the Scythian leader, replied to Darius:

> Persian, I have never yet run from any man in fear; and I am not doing so now from you. . . . If you want to know why I will not fight, I will tell you: in our country there are no towns and no cultivated land; fear of losing which, or seeing it ravaged, might indeed provoke us to hasty battle. If, however, you are determined on bloodshed . . . one thing there is for which we will fight—the tombs of our forefathers. Find those tombs, and try to wreck them, and you will soon know whether or not we are willing to stand up to you. . . . As for your being my master, I acknowledge no masters but God from whom I sprang. . . . I will send you no gifts of earth and water

> . . . and your claim to be my master is easily answered—be damned to you![52]

Apparently, the Persians did not find any Scythian tombs to wreck, for the cat-and-mouse game, in which the natives managed to avoid any pitched battles, continued for several more weeks. Frustration and an increasing lack of supplies for his men took their toll on Darius, who finally ordered a return to the Danube. No sooner had he crossed the river when he received the news that the Thracian tribes that had earlier submitted to him were now in rebellion. The Great King dispatched some eighty thousand troops, who quickly took back control of Thrace; and then he retired to Sardis, where he rested for a number of months before returning to the Persian heartland.

The Ionian Rebellion

It is likely that Darius interpreted his failure to conquer Scythia as a momentary disappointment rather than a defeat and that on the whole he saw the campaign as a productive one; after all, he had gained the extensive territories of Thrace, which became the new satrapy of Skudra, giving him a firm foothold in Europe. Undoubtedly he envisioned returning at a later date, although it remains unknown when he planned to renew his European ventures. As it happened, this decision was made for him by the Ionian Greeks, who viewed the results of the Scythian expedition much differently than he. During the campaign he had relied on soldiers from his subject cities in Ionia to build a bridge of boats across the Danube and to guard

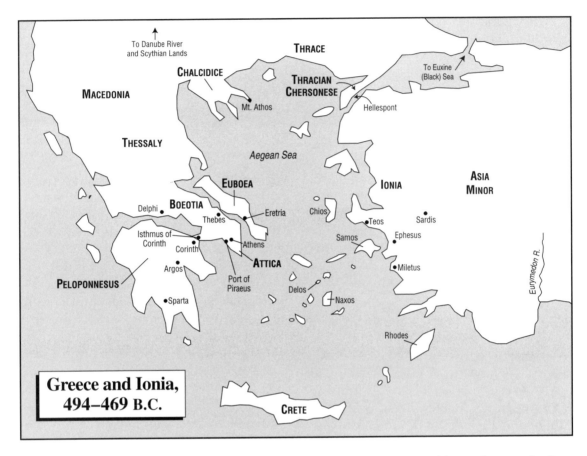

**Greece and Ionia,
494–469 B.C.**

that bridgehead while he was in the steppes. They had remained loyal in his absence, refusing to give in to Scythian pressure to destroy the bridge. From these events, classical scholar John Warry points out,

> both Darius and the Ionian Greeks drew mistaken conclusions. Darius assumed that in [the] future he could rely on the unswerving loyalty of the Ionians, and the Ionian Greeks, [concluding] that the Persians had been worsted by the Scythians, judged that the time was close when they themselves might with impunity and fair prospects [of success] raise a revolt against their Persian overlord.[53]

The Ionians had long dreamed of regaining their freedom. But their chances of doing so had been slim, mainly because they had continued to display the same disunity and lack of leadership that had ensured their subjugation decades earlier. This situation finally changed in 499 with the rise to prominence of Aristagoras, a distinguished citizen of Miletus, the strongest and most prosperous city of Ionia. Proving himself to be the right leader at the right time, he inspired the Ionians, secretly organized them, and coordinated the first stage of their revolt against Darius. All through Ionia, pro-Persian Greek leaders were deposed and replaced by rebel patriots.

Aristagoras was well aware that the rebellion would provoke a military response from the Great King and that the Ionians would be in for the fight of their lives; so to bolster his forces he immediately sought aid from the leading mainland Greek city-states. Because Sparta's army was the most formidable, it seemed logical to approach the Spartans first. Tempted by promises of acquiring Persian gold and other valuables from Susa, the Spartan king, Cleomenes, seemed on the verge of agreeing to lead his army into Persia. But then Aristagoras let it slip that Susa was a three-month journey from Sardis. Still reluctant to travel too far from home, the Spartans, as they had in the days of Cyrus the Great, refused to get involved in Ionia's troubles.

Aristagoras next tried Athens, Greece's acknowledged cultural leader, which had in the preceding decade instituted the world's first democracy. Every free adult Athenian male had the right to speak out and to vote on new laws and policies at meetings of the local assembly; and in yearly elections, the citizens chose three archons, or administrators, to run the government and ten military generals, the *strategoi*, to command the army. It was to this democratic citizenry that Aristagoras appealed, pointing out, according to Herodotus,

> that Miletus had been founded by Athenian settlers, so it was only natural that the Athenians, powerful as they were, should help her in her need. Indeed, so anxious was he to get Athenian aid, that he promised everything that came into his head, until at last he succeeded. Apparently it is easier to impose upon a crowd

than upon an individual, for Aristagoras, who had failed to impose upon Cleomenes, succeeded with thirty thousand Athenians.[54]

Disaster at Lade

The elated Aristagoras returned to Ionia with the reassuring news that Athens had agreed to help the rebels. Moreover, one of Athens's allies, Eretria, located on the large island of Euboea along Greece's east coast, had also agreed to send aid. Encouraged, early in 498 the Ionians grew bolder, forcing Darius's local officials to flee inland to Sardis and clashing openly with small groups of Persian soldiers. The rebellion even reached northward into Thrace, where the Greeks of that region also threw off the Persian yoke.

After the arrival of twenty ships from Athens and five from Eretria laden with troops and supplies, the rebels grew even more brazen, and also more than a little overconfident. A small raiding party of Milesians and Athenians, commanded by Aristagoras, descended on Sardis itself and within minutes set the city ablaze. The nearby large Persian garrison was alerted and, to the raiders' surprise, suddenly counterattacked. Unprepared to fight a major battle, the Greeks retreated; but their flight did not save them, for the Persian troops gave chase, cornered them near the seacoast, and, after some desperate fighting, overwhelmed them. While the Milesian survivors escaped to their city, the Athenian and Eretrian commanders decided that their own best strategy was to return to Greece while they still could. Thus, despite Aristagoras's fervent appeals the mainlanders abandoned Ionia to fight its own battles.

But if Athens and Eretria believed that withdrawing from the conflict at this early stage would prevent Darius from retaliating against them, they were mistaken. He was a proud, strong-willed ruler who had on many occasions demonstrated his ability to crush rebellions and to punish harshly those who had defied or insulted him. Clearly, in his mind the rebellious Ionians had defied him; and their mainland accomplices had insulted him by interfering in his empire's affairs. The burning of Sardis enraged him and he vowed that he would first put down the rebels, and then punish the upstart Athenians and Eretrians. Herodotus recorded that the Great King

asked who the Athenians were, and then, on being told, called for his bow. He took it, set an arrow on the string, shot it up into the air and cried: "Grant, O God, that I may punish the Athenians." Then he commanded one of his servants to repeat to him the words, "Master, remember the Athenians," three times, whenever he sat down to dinner.[55]

True to his vow, in the following four years Darius slowly but methodically surrounded and overcame the Ionian cities. The strategic potential of the navy that his predecessor Cambyses had created almost three decades before now became fully realized as Persian fleets seized control of

Athens's magnificent Acropolis, featuring the famous Parthenon, temple of the goddess Athena, as it looked after being rebuilt in the wake of the Persian wars.

the eastern Aegean, trapping the rebels between the sea and Darius's land armies. In 494 the Ionians made a desperate last stand in a huge sea battle fought near the tiny island of Lade, not far from Miletus; but their old disunity once more set in and the result was disaster. Some of the rebel ships turned and fled just after the fighting began and, seeing their escape, many others followed suit. A few ships, notably from Miletus and the islands of Chios and Samos, remained and fought gallantly, but the odds against them were too great and they suffered total defeat.[56]

The great city of Miletus was now nearly defenseless against Darius's forces. Herodotus described how the victorious Persians

> invested [surrounded] Miletus by land and sea. They dug saps [tunnels] under the walls, brought up rams of all kinds, and, five years after the revolt of Aristagoras, overwhelmed it. . . . Most of the [Milesian] men were killed by the Persians. . . . The women and children were made slaves, and . . . the men in the city whose lives were spared were sent as prisoners to Susa; Darius did them no harm, and settled them in Ampe, on the Persian Gulf, near the mouth of the Tigris.[57]

In the months that followed, the other Ionian cities also felt Darius's wrath. On rebellious islands such as Chios and Lesbos, thousands of Persian soldiers joined hands and marched from shore to shore, netting and capturing entire populations. Many cities were burned. And an unknown number of Greek children were taken back to Susa and other Persian centers; the boys were made into eunuchs (castrated) to serve at the royal court and

the girls became part of the king's harem. Darius's harsh treatment of the Ionians was clearly designed to discourage any further rebellions in the region.

The Fall of Eretria

Crushing Ionia did not fully satisfy the Great King's thirst for revenge, however; there were still the impudent Athenians and Eretrians to deal with. To that end he commanded Mardonius, a young nobleman who had recently wed Darius's daughter, the princess Artozostre, to launch an expedition. In 493 Mardonius led a Persian army from Asia Minor into Thrace, while a large Persian fleet sailed along the Aegean coast to supply and reinforce him. His first order of business was to reconquer Thrace, a task he easily accomplished in only a few months. He next planned to march southward along the mainland coast and burn and pillage Athens and Eretria as a punishment for their role in the Ionian revolt, a move that would also give Persia a strategic foothold in southern Greece. This plan was foiled, however, when an unexpected violent storm struck the invading fleet near Mt. Athos, on the Mt. Athos peninsula (the easternmost finger of the larger Chalcidic peninsula). According to Herodotus's account, the

> violent northerly gale . . . proved too much for the ships to cope with. A great many of them were driven ashore and wrecked on Athos—indeed, reports say that something like three hundred were lost with over twenty thousand men. The sea in the neighborhood of Athos

is full of monsters [sharks], so that those of the ships' companies who were not dashed to pieces on the rocks, were seized and devoured. Others, unable to swim, were drowned; others, again, died of the cold.[58]

Without the fleet, the Persian land army could not long sustain itself and Darius had no choice but to recall Mardonius and his forces.

But the mainland Greeks had not escaped the Great King's wrath, for he almost immediately began preparing another expedition against them. This time, he placed his forces under the command of Datis, a capable Median general, and Artaphernes, Darius's own nephew. The new plan was to avoid the potential costly delays of an overland march by assembling a strike force and sailing it directly across the Aegean to the target cities. In the spring of 490, Datis and Artaphernes arrived in Cilicia, in southern Asia Minor, and oversaw the loading of hundreds of ships and troop transports. In all, they had about sixty-five thousand men, of whom perhaps twenty thousand were sailors and supply personnel and the rest combat troops. When the armada was ready, it moved west along the coast, passing north of the large island of Rhodes; swung northwest to Samos; crossed a stretch of open sea to the island of Naxos, where the Persians burned the principal city; and finally headed northwest again, straight for Eretria.

As the Persians approached, people from the surrounding countryside crammed behind Eretria's defensive walls. The Greeks watched fearfully while Datis's and Artaphernes' soldiers, clad in their uniforms of purple and other bright colors, surrounded the city. "For six days," writes Herodotus, "fighting continued with many killed on both sides; then, on the seventh [day], two well-known Eretrians . . . betrayed the town to the enemy."[59] These two men, democrats who had long been bickering with members of the local conservative party, believed that the Persians would reward their action by putting their own party in power. But they were sadly mistaken. The invaders promptly burned the city and carried off the surviving inhabitants as prisoners.[60]

Encounter at Marathon

With the destruction of Eretria, Datis and Artaphernes had accomplished half of their mission. They were confident that their second objective—the subjugation of Athens—would be reached just as smoothly. Setting sail from Euboea in early September, they made the short journey to the shores of the Athenian territory of Attica, erecting their camp on the eastern edge of the flat plain of Marathon. Their initial strategy was apparently to march overland to Athens, some twenty-six miles distant, sack the city, and establish a Persian base in Attica.

But to the Persian commanders' surprise, an obstacle stood in their path. Athens's entire citizen-militia of some nine thousand hoplites, reinforced by six hundred hoplites from the tiny city-state of Plataea, located on Attica's northern border, had assembled on the western edge of the plain, blocking the road to Athens. Greek hoplites were heavily armored infantry soldiers who carried thrusting spears and short swords. They fought in a special formation called a

The Battle of Marathon

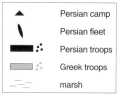

▲	Persian camp
╲	Persian fleet
▬ ∴	Persian troops
▬ ∴	Greek troops
---	marsh

These diagrams show a plausible reconstruction of the approximate stages of the battle, based on historical accounts, such as that of Herodotus, and archaeological studies of the site.

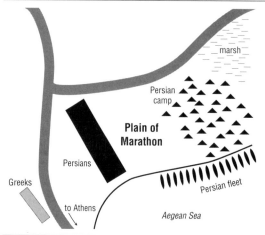

1. The Persians land at Marathon in early September 490 B.C., make camp, and prepare to take the nearby road to Athens; the Greeks occupy the high ground near the road; on the morning of September 12, the Greeks descend onto the plain about a mile from the Persian lines and prepare to attack.

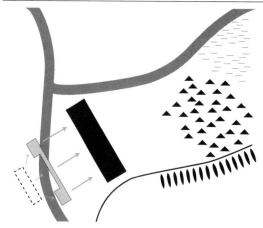

2. Miltiades, the chief Athenian general, extends his phalanx to match the length of the Persian lines in order to avoid an enemy flanking maneuver; to do so he must thin the center of his formation from a depth of 8–10 ranks to 2–4; the Plataeans are positioned on the left wing; the Greeks advance until they are in range of the Persian archers, then charge at a run, smashing with devastating force into the Persian lines.

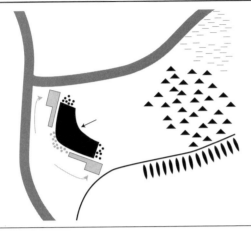

3. As the battle rages, the Persian front ranks manage to penetrate the weak Greek center; but at the same time the Greek wings steamroll over their opponents and then begin to wheel inward, enveloping the enemy center and sending a wave of fear through the Persian ranks.

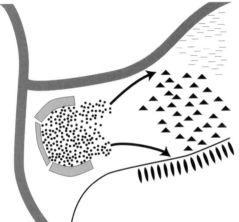

4. Many Persians flee the field in disarray, some toward their ships, others toward the imagined safety of the marshes behind their camp; meanwhile, the Greeks, having enveloped the leading Persian contingents, proceed to annihilate all within reach.

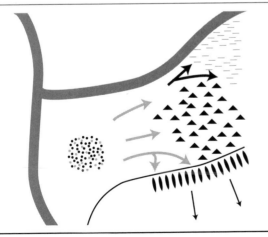

5. The Greeks pursue the fleeing enemy; the fighting continues in the marshes and also on the beaches, where the Athenian war archon Callimachus is killed; the surviving Persians escape on their ships, although the Greeks manage to capture seven of the vessels.

The Athenian and Plataean hoplites drive the Persians to the beaches in the last stage of the Marathon battle. Here, according to Herodotus, Athens's war archon, Callimachus, and the brother of the famous dramatist Aeschylus met their deaths.

phalanx, which had developed in mainland Greece in the eighth and early seventh centuries B.C. A typical phalanx was composed of eight ranks, or rows, of hoplites; when standing in close order, their uplifted shields formed a formidable unbroken protective barrier. As this formation marched toward an enemy, the men in the front rank jabbed their spears at their opponents while the hoplites in the rear ranks pushed at their comrades' backs, giving the whole unit a tremendous and lethal forward momentum.

The Greek phalanx was as yet untested in a large open battle with Persian troops, whose own reputation for fighting skill and ferocity was widespread. So Datis and Artaphernes had little or no idea of the destructive potential of the small army they now faced. They were certainly surprised when the Greeks, despite their greatly inferior numbers, boldly launched a frontal attack on the morning of September 12. "The Persians," Herodotus recalls,

> seeing the attack developing at the double, prepared to meet it, thinking it suicidal madness for the Athenians to risk an assault with so small a force—rushing in with no support

from either cavalry or archers. . . . Nevertheless, the Athenians came on.[61]

In the bloody battle that followed, the Greek hoplites and their phalanx proved more disciplined and far deadlier than the Persian myriads, who eventually fell back and fled in confusion to the beaches. The Greeks gave chase and managed to capture seven ships before the fleet escaped. Datis and Artaphernes, having lost over 6,400 men (compared to only 192 Athenians killed), soon scrubbed their mission and returned to Asia Minor, where they dispatched a messenger carrying the bad news, along with their excuses, to Darius.

In the wake of the Persian retreat, the Greeks celebrated in a triumphant chorus that has echoed mightily in the subsequent literature and folklore of Western civilization; for to them, the victory was one of epic proportions. By contrast, from the Persians' viewpoint the loss at Marathon was but a tiny dent in their invincible empire's armor. Undaunted, and still contemptuous of "crude," "inferior," and "insolent" Greece, they would soon return to its shores, this time with the largest invasion force the world had yet seen.

Chapter

6 An Enormous Potential Unfulfilled: Xerxes Versus the Greeks

Unbeknownst to the Greeks as they joyously celebrated their victory over Datis and Artaphernes, in faraway Susa the man who lorded over much of the known world was already drawing new plans against them. Herodotus tells us that

> when the news of the battle of Marathon reached Darius . . . his anger against Athens already great enough on account of the assault on Sardis, was even greater, and he was more than ever determined to make war on Greece. Without loss of time he dispatched couriers to the various states under his dominion with orders to raise an army much larger than before; and also warships, transports, horses, and grain. So the royal command went round; and all Asia was in an uproar for three years, with the best men being enrolled in the army for the invasion of Greece.[62]

But Darius was not destined to achieve his revenge on Athens and Eretria and to see his empire expand into the unknown wilds of Europe; late in 486 B.C., after a highly productive reign of thirty-six years, he died. Fortunately for the empire, he had already designated a successor. Darius had three sons by his first wife, the daughter of one of his fellow conspirators in the assassination of Gautama, and four more sons by his second wife, Atossa, daughter of the already legendary Cyrus the Great. Of the two wives, Atossa wielded the most influence on the king and his court; and so the eldest of her brood, Xerxes (pronounced ZERK-seez), was chosen to inherit the throne. A

Xerxes I, who succeeded his father, Darius, as king of Persia. According to most ancient accounts, the son, though largely an able ruler, lacked the father's wisdom and tact.

tablet inscription found at Persepolis reads: "Darius also had other sons, but by the will of Ahura-Mazda he made me the greatest after himself. When Darius my father passed away, by the will of Ahura-Mazda I became king."[63]

At first, Xerxes expressed little interest in pursuing his father's European plans. But then some of the new king's advisers began to work on him. His brother-in-law Mardonius, for example, argued that the Athenians must not go unpunished and added that Europe was a beautiful, bountiful region ripe for Persian exploitation. Eventually, the king expressed great enthusiasm for the venture, stating to his followers:

> I have found a way to win for Persia not glory only but a country as large and as rich as our own . . . and at the same time to get satisfaction and revenge. . . . I will bridge the Hellespont and march an army . . . into Greece, and punish the Athenians for the outrage they committed upon my father and upon us. . . . We shall so extend the empire of Persia that its boundaries will be God's own sky, so that the sun will not look down upon any land beyond the boundaries of what is ours. With your help I shall pass through Europe from end to end and make it all one country.[64]

Having made up his mind, Xerxes eventually completed his father's military preparations and led an immense combined land and naval invasion force against Greece. As it turned out, this herculean effort did profoundly affect the futures of both Europe and Persia, though decidedly not in the ways the new Great King had intended.

A Formidable Military Leader

However great Xerxes' dreams of European conquest, problems closer to home compelled him to postpone the Greek expedition for several years. Shortly before Darius's death, Egypt had risen in rebellion and the new king's first priority was to bring this valuable asset back into the imperial fold. Xerxes completed the task by January 484. To demonstrate that he would tolerate no more such insurrections, he confiscated many of the lands belonging to the local temples and imposed stricter rules and penalties on the natives. He also appointed as Egyptian satrap someone he felt he could trust implicitly—his brother Achaemenes (named after the dynastic founder).

No sooner had Xerxes quelled this challenge to the central authority when another flared up, this time in Babylon. The Great King was in Ecbatana in 483 when news reached him that his Babylonian satrap, Zopryas, had been murdered and that a man named Shamasheriba had declared himself "king of Babylon." This revolt was short-lived, however. Xerxes dispatched his finest general, Megabyzus, who quickly recaptured the city and, following the king's orders, imposed on it harsh penalties. Babylon's splendid outer fortifications were torn down, its temples and statues of local gods demolished, and the estates of its wealthiest citizens confiscated and distributed to native Persians.

Xerxes' handling of the two rebellions showed that he was a formidable military leader who would brook no disobedience and act swiftly against transgressors. Another strength he shared with his father

An artist's conception of the bridge of boats Xerxes ordered built across the Hellespont. When a storm damaged the structure, the Persian monarch ordered his men to flog the waters in a public display of punishment.

was his patient and thorough approach to war preparations, as demonstrated by the ongoing military buildup for the Greek invasion. Far in advance of the army's arrival, engineers and laborers constructed impressive boat bridges over the Hellespont to facilitate the crossing into Europe. "The method was as follows," Herodotus reports:

> Galleys and triremes [warships] were lashed together to support the bridges—360 vessels for the one on the Black Sea side, and 314 for the other. They were moored slantwise to the Black Sea and at right angles to the Hellespont, in order to lessen the strain on the cables. Specially heavy anchors were laid out both upstream and downstream. . . . Once the vessels were in position, the cables were hauled taut by wooden winches ashore. . . . The flax and papyrus cables were of the same thickness and quality, but the flax was the heavier. . . . The next operation was to cut planks equal in length to the width of the floats, lay them edge to edge over

the taut cables, and then bind them together on their upper surface. That done, brushwood was put on top and spread evenly, with a layer of soil, trodden hard, over all. Finally a paling [fence] was constructed along each side, high enough to prevent horses and mules from seeing over and taking fright at the water.[65]

Even more ingenious and impressive was a project begun over two years before the bridge. Demonstrating his foresight, Xerxes ordered a canal dug through the Mt. Athos peninsula in the northern Aegean, eliminating the chance that another fleet might be lost rounding the promontory south of the mountain. In this endeavor the king may also have been thinking ahead to the day when such a waterway would facilitate trade to and from his Greek satrapy; as Herodotus points out, for the purpose of attack alone an easier method of avoiding the promontory was available: "There would have been no difficulty at all in getting the ships hauled across the isthmus on land; yet he ordered the construction of a

Xerxes' Canal

In his Histories, *Herodotus gives the following description of the construction of Xerxes' canal across the Mt. Athos peninsula.*

"The ground was divided into sections for the men of the various nations [under Persian dominion], on a line taped across the isthmus. . . . When the trench reached a certain depth, the laborers at the bottom carried on with the digging and passed the soil up to the others above them, who stood on terraces and passed it on to another lot, still higher up, until it reached the men at the top, who carried it away and dumped it. All the nations except the Phoenicians had their work doubled by the sides falling in, as they naturally would, since they made the cutting the same width at the top as it was intended to be at the bottom. But the Phoenicians, in this as in Xerxes' other works, gave a signal example of their skill. They, in the section allotted to them, took out a trench double the width prescribed for the actual finished canal, and by digging at a slope contracted [narrowed] it as they got further down, until at the bottom their section was the same width as the rest."

channel for the sea broad enough for two warships to be rowed abreast."[66]

Less Compassionate than His Father

But whereas the new king was an efficient ruler and capable military planner, he was more arrogant, tactless, and temperamental than his father had been. Among the seemingly childish and mean-spirited acts attributed to Xerxes were his reactions to the news that a sudden storm had severely damaged his boat bridge at the Hellespont. He was, as Herodotus tells it,

very angry when he learned of the disaster, and gave orders that the Hellespont should receive three hundred lashes. . . . He also sent people to brand it with hot irons. He certainly instructed the men with the whips to utter, as they wielded them . . . "You salt and bitter stream, your master lays this punishment upon you for injuring him, who never injured you. But Xerxes the King will cross you, with or without your permission. No man sacrifices to you, and you deserve the neglect by your acid and muddy waters." In addition to punishing the Hellespont Xerxes gave orders that the men responsible for building the bridges should have their heads cut off.[67]

Some scholars have suggested that the punishment of the waterway was religiously motivated, since according to Zoroastrian beliefs brackish waters were the result of defilement by the evil Ahriman; or that the act was designed to boost morale among the Great King's many non-Persian soldiers by showing that he held power even over natural forces like the winds and waves. But these suppositions do not explain Xerxes' cruel beheading of his engineers, who were scarcely to blame for the storm.

Nor do they account for or excuse an incident that occurred after the boat bridge had been rebuilt. As the army was leaving Sardis for the Hellespont, one of the king's Lydian subjects, a man named Pythius, requested that Xerxes excuse the eldest of his five sons from military service so that if all five died on the campaign, his family line would not be wiped out. To this reasonable request, the king responded with an outburst of rage and spite. According to Herodotus, he ordered men to "find Pythius's eldest son and cut him in half and put the two halves one on each side of the road, for the army to march out between them. The order was performed. And now between the halves of the young man's body the advance of the army began."[68] Such arbitrary cruelties suggest that Xerxes was a far less compassionate ruler than either Darius or Cyrus.

In the area of military logistics, however, Xerxes far outdistanced his illustrious predecessors. The invasion force that approached the Hellespont in the spring of 480 dwarfed all others in ancient times.

Xerxes holds court. After a swift, direct attack across the Aegean failed on the plain of Marathon, the new king decided to gradually advance a land army through Thrace and northern Greece.

It consisted of an estimated 200,000 combat infantry and cavalry, 800 to 1,000 ships manned by at least 150,000 oarsmen and sailors, and a huge following of support personnel and camp followers numbering perhaps as many as 300,000.[69] The enormity of the threat this host posed to Greece is emphasized by the puny size of the Greek armies of the day. Even the most populous city-states (Athens heading the list) were able to field armies of only a few thousand men, and most could muster no more than a few hundred. It is no wonder, then, that a wave of apprehension and fear swept through Greece as the mighty Persian host entered Europe.

Herodotus describes the fateful Hellespontine crossing this way:

> The infantry and cavalry went over by the upper bridge—the one nearer the Black Sea; the pack animals and underlings by the lower one towards the Aegean. The first to cross were the Ten Thousand [Immortals], all with wreaths on their heads, and these were followed by the mass of troops of all the nations. Their crossing occupied the whole of the first day. On the next day . . . came the sacred horses and the sacred chariot, and after them Xerxes himself with his spearmen and

Xerxes' ships cross the Hellespont in this fanciful German drawing from 1633.

his thousand horsemen. The remainder of the army brought up the rear, and at the same time the ships moved over to the opposite shore. . . . The crossing occupied seven days and seven nights without a break.[70]

The Persians March on Athens

As Xerxes' massive army moved through northern Greece, most of the city-states in the region, fearing annihilation, submitted without a fight. This he expected, for the Greek advisers who accompanied him said that the more powerful states of southern Greece, especially Athens and Sparta, would be the most likely to resist. They also told him that the pass of Thermopylae, about a hundred miles northwest of Athens, was his best avenue through the mountains of central Greece because it was close enough to the sea to allow his troops easy access to their ships. When the Persians reached the pass in July 480, however, they found their way blocked by a small force of Greek hoplites.

The Greek fortification of Thermopylae had begun months before when, faced with the imminent invasion, representatives from thirty-one city-states met at Corinth, in the northern Peloponnesus. The object was for these states, who frequently quarreled and warred among themselves, to find some way of uniting and adopting a common defensive strategy. The Greek leaders, most prominent among them the dynamic Athenian politician Themistocles, knew that they would need a huge land force to oppose Xerxes' army and that assembling such a force from the many small and scattered city-states, if even feasible, would take time. It seemed more realistic to concentrate their efforts on destroying the Persian fleet. Without ships to supply and reinforce it, they correctly reasoned, the Persian army would be partially crippled. So the initial plan was for delaying tactics to keep Xerxes' troops in the north as long as possible while Themistocles and other admirals prepared a united Greek fleet.

The decision was made to fortify Thermopylae because it was very narrow, a stretch of it closing to just fifty feet. Herodotus comments, "The realization that the Persians would be unable, in the narrow pass, to use their cavalry or take advantage of their numbers, determined them [the Greeks] to make their stand at this point against the invader."[71] Taking charge of the operation, Sparta's king Leonidas marched north with three hundred handpicked men; and hoplites from other states joined him along the way, so that the total force that reached the pass numbered about seven thousand.

At first Xerxes was confident that his own huge forces would easily sweep the tiny Greek band from the pass, allowing him to march directly on Athens. But the armament, fighting prowess, and sheer determination of the hoplites, as was the case at Marathon, proved unexpectedly formidable. Diodorus's description of the first day of the fighting affords an idea of the Greeks' stunning initial success in the face of overwhelming odds:

The fight which followed was a fierce one, and since the barbarians [Persians] had the king as a witness of their valor and the Greeks kept in mind their liberty . . . it followed that the struggle was amazing. For since the men stood shoulder to shoulder . . . and the blows were struck in close combat, and the lines were densely packed, for a considerable time the battle was equally balanced. But . . . the Persians gradually gave way; for many of them were slain and not a few wounded. . . . At last, Xerxes, seeing that the entire area about the pass was strewn with dead bodies and that the Persians were not holding out against the . . . Greeks, sent forward the picked Persians known as the "Immortals," who were reputed to be preeminent among the entire host for their deeds of courage. But when these also fled after only a brief resistance, then at last, as night fell, they ceased from battle, the Persians having lost many dead and the Greeks a small number.[72]

When it looked as though the Greeks might be able to hold the pass indefinitely, Xerxes found another solution. He paid a local civilian a substantial sum of gold in exchange for showing his men a little-known goat path that led to a point behind the Greek position. When Leonidas learned that a large Persian force was closing in from the rear, he dismissed most of the united troops so as to spare them for future fighting; soon, he, his three hundred Spartans, and about a thousand other Greeks, having resolved to fight to the death, were surrounded and overwhelmed.

Xerxes now marched his forces southward unopposed. On or about September 17, 480, the Persians entered Athens, finding to their surprise that the city was largely deserted, the Athenians having just

Persian troops (in foreground) make little headway against the Spartans and other Greeks holding the pass of Thermopylae. Eventually, the pass fell through treachery.

evacuated to the nearby island of Salamis and other locations. A few diehards had barricaded themselves on the Acropolis, the city's central hill fortress, and Xerxes ordered a contingent of soldiers to remove them. When the defenders on the summit saw the Persians approaching, Herodotus writes,

> some leapt from the wall to their death, others sought sanctuary in the inner shrine of the temple; but the Persians . . . slaughtered those in the sanctuary. Having left not one of them alive, they

stripped the temple of its treasures and burned everything on the Acropolis. Xerxes, now absolute master of Athens, dispatched a rider to Susa with [the] news . . . of his success.[73]

Elated, the Great King felt that he had at last achieved his father's revenge for the burning of Sardis some eighteen years before.

Susa in Mourning

But the Great King's triumph was short-lived; for to his disappointment his brief occupation of the deserted city turned out to be the high point of the campaign. Despite his careful planning and the great size of his army and navy, a number of logistical and psychological factors greatly impeded his chances for success. First, the Greek hoplites consistently proved themselves superior to the Persian infantry-men, in part because the Greeks had more effective armor and shields, and also because they were better trained in combat at close quarters. In addition, the Greeks had a psychological edge because they were fighting for their liberty; unlike the Persian troops, whose lives were subject to the whims of an absolute monarch, most Greeks knew what it was like to be free and to control their own destiny. Defending their homeland and way of life, the hoplites fought desperately, often heroically. By contrast, the bulk of the Persian ranks were made up of conscripts from the empire's subject lands, many of whom felt little loyalty to the Great King and could not be counted on to fight enthusiastically for him.

These factors contributed heavily to the three major defeats Xerxes' forces suffered in the year following his entrance into Athens. The most decisive of these occurred in the bay of Salamis, a few miles southwest of Athens, where his fleet was crushed by an allied Greek effort directed by Themistocles. From a throne set up on a hill overlooking the bay, the Great King watched the struggle, which the Athenian playwright Aeschylus later captured in his play *The Persians*. A Persian messenger, having returned to Susa, describes the battle to the queen mother, Atossa:

> At once ship into ship battered its brazen beak. A Greek ship charged first, and chopped off the whole stern of a Persian galley. Then charge followed charge on every side. At first by its huge impetus our fleet withstood them. But soon, in that narrow space, our ships were jammed in hundreds; none could help another. They rammed each other with their prows of bronze; and some were stripped of every oar. Meanwhile the enemy came round us in a ring and charged. Our vessels heeled over; the sea was hidden, carpeted with wrecks and dead men; all the shores and reefs were full of dead. Then every ship we had broke rank and rowed for life. The Greeks seized fragments of wrecks and broken oars and hacked and stabbed at our men swimming in the sea. . . . The whole sea was one din of shrieks and dying groans, till night and darkness hid the scene.[74]

When the news of the disaster reached Susa, the first reaction was shock and disbelief; then thousands of people began openly wailing and tearing at their clothes, a traditional Persian expression of grief.

Susa and other cities in the Persian heartland remained in a state of mourning until Xerxes returned about a year later. Western sources have typically portrayed his departure for Sardis shortly after the Salamis episode as a cowardly retreat; but it is more likely that he viewed the defeat merely as a single setback in a campaign that he expected would be successful in the end. He did, after all, leave most of his land army in place, charging its commander, Mardonius, with the task of subjugating southern Greece. In fact, Mardonius urged the king to "go home" and promised, "I will make it my duty . . . to deliver Greece to you in chains."[75]

Xerxes was no doubt thoroughly surprised when the news came the following summer (479 B.C.) that the Greeks had almost completely destroyed Mardonius's army in a hard-fought battle near Plataea. Another Greek victory a few days later at Mycale, near Lade on the Ionian coast, seemed, for Xerxes, to add insult to injury. His loss of men and ships was now so great that he had no other choice but to abandon his European campaign. But it must be emphasized that the Persian Empire itself had not been defeated, nor even threatened with attack; Xerxes' failure in Greece, like his father's, was seen in Persia as an unfortunate but tempo-

The fearsome massed spears and shields of a Greek phalanx mow down a contingent of Persian soldiers who are little match for the highly armored and well-drilled hoplites.

The Slaughter in the Stockade

In his Library of History, *Diodorus includes this account of how, after fleeing the battlefield at Plataea and taking refuge in their stockaded camp, the survivors of Mardonius's army soon found themselves surrounded and besieged by the victorious Greek hoplites.*

"Both sides put up a vigorous contest, the barbarians [Persians] fighting bravely from the fortified positions they held and the Greeks storming the wooden walls, and many were wounded as they fought desperately, while not a few were also slain by the multitude of missiles [arrows, javelins, and rocks]. . . . The powerful onset of the Greeks could be withstood neither by the wall the Persians had erected nor by their great numbers. . . . In the end the Persians were overpowered, and they found no mercy even though they pled to be taken prisoner. For the Greek general, Pausanias [of Sparta], observing how superior the Persians were in number, took pains to prevent anything due to miscalculation from happening. . . . Consequently he had issued orders to take no man prisoner, and soon there were an incredible number of dead. And . . . when the Greeks had slaughtered more than one hundred thousand of the Persians, they reluctantly ceased slaying the enemy."

rary setback in the "rightful" and "inevitable" Persian conquest of the known world.

A Thorn in His Side

As it turned out, however, Xerxes' failure to mount a new expedition against Greece right away was a tactical blunder that both he and his successors would later pay for in Persian blood. The victories over Darius and Xerxes galvanized the Greeks, inspiring in them the belief that their own culture was superior and destined for great things. In the wake of the Persian retreat, Athens organized more than 150 city-states from the Greek mainland, Aegean islands, and Ionia into the Delian League, a political-military alliance designed on the one hand to defend Greece and on the other to go on the offensive against Persia.[76] The League quickly became a thorn in Xerxes' side. Although its operations were confined mainly to the coasts of Asia Minor and did not threaten Persia's overall stability, he was forced to send army after army into the area, thus wasting precious human and material resources that might have been better used elsewhere. What is

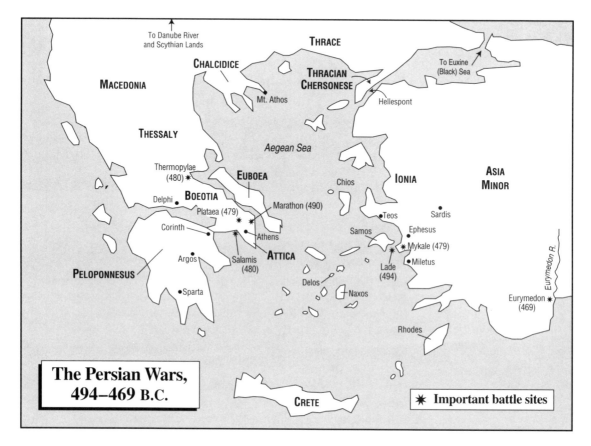

The Persian Wars,
494–469 B.C.

✳ Important battle sites

been better used elsewhere. What is more, the Greeks were consistently successful, their efforts culminating in a major victory over a large Persian force at the mouth of the Eurymedon River, in southern Asia Minor, in 469.

During these years, Xerxes fared little better in his domestic affairs. With the exception of the splendid additions he made to the still-growing royal palace complex at Persepolis, the remainder of his reign was undistinguished; wasting his energies in sordid court intrigues, he failed to fulfill the enormous political and military po-

tential he had inherited from Darius. In 465, Artabanus, the powerful captain of the royal guard, backed by the once trusted general Megabyzus, engineered a successful assassination plot. Soon afterward, the conspirators placed Xerxes' eighteen-year-old son, Artaxerxes, on the throne. They buried the slain king in a rock tomb near that of his father; but unlike Darius's final resting place, Xerxes' bore no elaborate inscriptions proclaiming his greatness, for he was the first Persian monarch who had failed to expand and significantly strengthen the empire.

Chapter

7 The Pale Shadow of a Great Empire: Persia's Decline and Fall

The vile manner of Xerxes' death and the sinister events of the months and years that followed it foreshadowed the decline and eventual fall of his empire. After his murder, the conspirators laid the blame on the eldest prince, named Darius after Xerxes' father, though the young man had had no hand in the deed. Darius was summarily executed to make way for the coronation of his younger brother Artaxerxes. The bloodletting did not end here, however. For several months, Artabanus ruled the empire by manipulating Artaxerxes, until the royal guardsman felt confident enough to kill the boy-king and openly usurp the throne; but the assassination attempt failed when Megabyzus stepped in and did away with the ambitious Artabanus. Artaxerxes then settled down to a long but lackluster reign. He proved a weak-willed, incompetent ruler who allowed his scheming, twisted, and bloodthirsty mother, Amestris, both to manipulate him and with impunity to murder and mutilate those she disliked.

The intrigue-filled reign of Artaxerxes in many ways typified those of most of his successors, who were largely self-absorbed, second-rate leaders. They were unable or unwilling to deal effectively with some of the serious problems the empire faced, among them the disruptions and chaos caused by frequent internal power struggles; increasing discontent among the subject peoples, especially those far from the Persian heartland; the delegation by the kings of too much authority to underlings who were often interested only in increasing their own wealth and power; more and more military use of paid Greek mercenaries, whose loyalty to Persia was lukewarm at best; and a general loss of interest in expanding the realm. It is not surprising that under these mediocre rulers the Persian Empire's political stability, structural integrity, and reputation as a great military power steadily deteriorated.

In the end, then, it was a much weaker and less efficient empire, a pale shadow of the one Cyrus and Darius had ruled, that had to face the greatest crisis in Persia's history. The challenge came in the late 330s B.C. from its longtime nemesis, Greece. As allied Greek forces under the brilliant leadership of Alexander the Great crushed the empire's armies and swept through its heartland to the very gates of Susa and Persepolis, many Persians realized, too late, that the earlier failure to subdue and absorb Greece had been a fatal error.

Greed, Cruelty, and Decay

That the process of decay and decline was at first subtle and gradual is illustrated by the fact that in the early years of Artaxerxes' reign the empire was still a world power to be reckoned with. Despite his weak leadership and the unseemly affairs of his royal court, many of his satraps and generals were competent, talented individuals who kept the realm on a relatively even keel.

A clear example of Persia's continued potent military potential was its handling

Persia's King Artaxerxes I, successor to Xerxes, was determined to drive the Greeks out of Egypt and reclaim that land as part of his empire. Thanks to the capable Persian general Megabyzus, Artaxerxes succeeded.

of a major rebellion by Egypt in 460. According to Diodorus:

> The inhabitants of Egypt . . . decided to strike for their liberty. . . . Mustering an army, they revolted from the Persians, and after expelling the Persians whose duty it was to collect the tribute from Egypt, they set up as king a man named Inaros. He at first recruited soldiers from the native Egyptians, but afterwards he gathered also mercenaries from the other nations and amassed a considerable army. He dispatched ambassadors also to the Athenians to effect an alliance. . . . And the Athenians, having decided that it was to their advantage to humble the Persians as far as they could . . . voted to send three hundred triremes to the aid of the Egyptians.[77]

In about 457 in the Nile delta, the combined Egyptian-Athenian army met a Persian force led by Xerxes' brother (and Artaxerxes' uncle) Achaemenes. Thanks to the fighting prowess of the Greek hoplites, the rebels almost completely wiped out the Persians, killing Achaemenes in the process. Afterward, the Athenians speedily stormed and occupied Memphis. For a while, it looked as though Egypt had finally gained permanent freedom from Persian domination.

However, in the following year the capable Megabyzus arrived on the scene with a huge army, delivered the rebels a shattering defeat, and captured Inaros. In the face of the onslaught, the Athenians were forced to retreat to a nearby Nile island; there, after a desperate and courageous defense lasting more than a year, they were overwhelmed, losing two hundred ships and some forty thousand men.

Economic Decline

In this excerpt from his History of the Persian Empire, *A. T. Olmstead explains how excessive taxation and the hoarding of precious metals, especially gold and silver, led to inflation and thereby contributed to Persia's slow but steady economic decline during its final century.*

"From the satrapies a constant stream of silver flowed in[to the royal treasury]. . . . Little of this vast sum was ever returned to the satrapies. It was the custom to melt down the gold and silver and to pour it into jars which were then broken and the bullion stored. Only a small portion was ever coined, and then usually for the purchase of foreign soldiers or foreign statesmen. Thus, despite the precious metals newly mined, the empire was rapidly drained of its gold and silver. . . . For a time credit made possible a continuance of business, but the . . . demand for actual silver in the payment of taxes drove the landlords in increasing numbers to the loan sharks. . . . As coined money became a rarity, hoarded by the loan sharks [as well as by the government], credit increased the [rate of] inflation, and rapidly rising prices made the situation still more intolerable."

Persia's imperial fist now closed tighter than ever around Egypt.

The crushing of the rebellion, accompanied by a rare event—the defeat of a Greek army by Persian soldiers—greatly increased Artaxerxes' prestige and that of his empire. But the credit for the victory belonged to Megabyzus, not to the king. The reality was that Persia's power and dominion over its vast realm could be maintained only so long as strong generals like Megabyzus led the armies and remained loyal to the central authority. Megabyzus himself demonstrated how fragile the empire's foundations actually were when he suddenly rebelled in the 440s.[78] In repelling two royal armies sent against him, he showed that without him the Persian military was far less effective; and in even-

tually obtaining a full pardon from Artaxerxes, he revealed the feeble nature of Persia's top leadership, for there is little doubt that under Darius or Xerxes, Megabyzus would have been executed.

The empire's central authority continued to weaken under Artaxerxes' successor. When the king died in 424 after a reign of forty-one years, a new power struggle for the throne erupted. First, his son Xerxes II became king; but only months later another son, Soghdianos, murdered Xerxes; soon after that a third son, Ochus, pushed aside Soghdianos. Ochus then ascended the throne in 423, assuming the title of Darius II. Little if anything good can be said about his reign. There were frequent insurrections, usually supported by contingents of Greek mercenaries, and at the royal court the degeneration of the high moral ideals of Cyrus and the first Darius continued. The depths of greed and cruelty to which the high nobility had sunk are illustrated by the episode in which Terituchmes, the new Great King's son-in-law, plotted to seize the throne. When the coup failed, Terituchmes was killed, after which the queen, Parysatis, had his mistress and all of his relatives, despite their innocence, buried alive.

Cyrus the Younger and the Disaster at Cunaxa

When Darius II died in 404, yet another royal power struggle ensued, this time resulting in the most dangerous and damaging rebellion the Persian monarchy ever faced. Darius's eldest son, Arsaces, was chosen to succeed him as Artaxerxes II, much to the regret and anger of the second son, Cyrus (whom the Greeks called Cyrus the Younger to differentiate him from Cyrus the Great). Four years before, through the influence of the queen mother, Parysatis, who favored him over Arsaces, Cyrus, then only sixteen years old, had been granted most of the satrapies of Asia Minor. This had greatly reduced the power of Tissaphernes, an able governor who had held sway over the area for many years.

Now, with his brother about to be crowned at Pasargadae, Cyrus made his first attempt to grab the throne. He boldly prepared to kill Arsaces during the coronation ceremony and would likely have succeeded had not Tissaphernes uncovered the plot at the last moment. The new

king wanted Cyrus immediately executed, but Parysatis intervened. According to Plutarch in his biography of Artaxerxes II, she "clasped [Cyrus] in her arms, and, entwining him with the tresses of her hair, joined his neck close to her own, and by her bitter lamentation and intercession to Artaxerxes for him, succeeded in saving his life."[79] Cyrus received the king's reluctant pardon and was allowed to return to his western satrapies.

Artaxerxes' clemency proved to be a serious mistake, however. Once back in Asia Minor, Cyrus began preparing a major rebellion, managing in the next two years to raise a formidable army consisting of about a hundred thousand natives from his provinces and some thirteen thousand Greek mercenaries. The Greeks were led by an experienced Spartan general named Clearchus. In 401 Cyrus marched his forces southward through Cilicia and Syria, and then westward toward the Euphrates. He had fully expected Artaxerxes to back down before the rebel host; but at Cunaxa, about fifty miles from Babylon, the king and Tissaphernes surprised Cyrus with an even bigger army. According to the eyewitness account of Xenophon, who fought under Clearchus, the opening of the battle favored the rebels, as the Greek phalanx charged the Persian left wing with devastating effect:

> The two lines were hardly six or seven hundred yards apart when the Greeks began to chant the battle hymn and moved against the enemy. . . . Then all together broke into a ringing cheer, "Eleleu, eleleu!" [the war cry] and all charged at the double. . . . They also beat their spears on their shields to scare the [Persian] horses. Before one

Greeks and Persians grapple in the battle of Cunaxa, fought near Babylon in 401 B.C. This momentous event was immediately followed by another—the legendary "March of the Ten Thousand."

shot [of arrows] reached them [the Greeks], the Persians turned and fled. At once the Greeks pursued . . . but shouted to each other, "Don't run races! Keep your line!"[80]

Encouraged by the Greeks' successful maneuver, Cyrus, who commanded a cavalry unit in the center of his battle line, launched a bold charge directly into the Persian center. Cutting through a much larger force of enemy horsemen, he reached Artaxerxes himself and in triumph screamed, "I see the man!" Before the king could react, Cyrus hurled a javelin, unhorsing his brother; but that was as close as the would-be usurper ever got to the royal purple, for the king's followers quickly moved in and killed Cyrus.

The only slightly wounded Artaxerxes ordered Tissaphernes to send the bulk of his troops against Cyrus's native levies; learning that their leader was dead, the rebels quickly fell into disorder and retreated. Clearchus and his Greeks later returned from their pursuit to find the battle lost.

The March of the Ten Thousand

In the days that followed, an uneasy truce prevailed between the huge Persian host and the small Greek band. Then, after a series of preliminary negotiations, Tissaphernes invited Clearchus and the other

Greek leaders to a peace conference and treacherously murdered them. On hearing of this outrage, the Greeks defiantly chose new leaders, among them Xenophon. They were determined to march homeward but, as Xenophon later wrote, they realized the daunting dangers they faced:

> After the captains had been seized, and the officers and men who were their escort had been cut down, the Greeks were . . . full of anxiety. There they were at the king's door, and round them everywhere so many nations and cities of the enemy. No one now would provide them a market; they were distant from Greece more than a thousand miles, with no guide for the road. Impassable rivers crossed the homeward way, and they had been deserted even by the natives who had come up country with Cyrus.[81]

Despite these obstacles, the Greeks struck out toward the northwest, initiating the now famous "March of the Ten Thousand" that Xenophon later immortalized in his *Anabasis*. After enduring incredible hardships, including often freezing weather and almost constant attacks by Persian troops and fierce hill tribesmen, the Greeks made it to the shores of the Black Sea and eventually their homes. Their harrowing adventure and ultimate success would prove crucial to Greek-Persian military relations in the coming years. They had shown first that, even in the midst of Persia's heartland, Persian troops could not match Greek hoplites. Second, if a Greek army as small and ill supplied as Clearchus's could fight its way through Asia and emerge in one piece, what damage might a far larger and better-supplied Greek force inflict on Persia? For

many Greeks, the events of Cunaxa and its aftermath became, in a sense, a military manual on how to defeat the Persians.

A Troubled, Fragile Empire

Not surprisingly, the official Persian line interpreted these same events differently. According to the Great King's propaganda, he had bravely driven an invading Greek army out of his homeland. Of course, Artaxerxes knew better, for he had himself witnessed the terrifying charge of the hoplites at Cunaxa and realized that he had to do whatever he could to reduce the threat of Greek attacks on his empire. When the Spartan king Agesilaus, partly inspired by the exploits of Xenophon's Ten Thousand, began raiding the satrapies of Asia Minor in 396, Artaxerxes paid large sums of gold to a coalition of Greek states, including Athens and Thebes, to attack Sparta; this had the desired effect of forcing Agesilaus to abandon his conquests and return to defend his homeland.[82]

Later, in 387, the Great King took the further step of concluding the Peace of Antalcidas (or "King's Peace"), to which the major Greek states subscribed. The terms were favorable for Persia: All of Asia Minor, including the Ionian Greek cities, was deemed Persian territory; at the same time, the Great King agreed to recognize the sovereignty of the mainland Greek states and to stay out of their affairs as long as they stayed out of his. For the first time in many years, Persia's western border appeared safe.

But Artaxerxes did not fare nearly so well in many other parts of his empire. As

Freedom at Last

Here, from his thrilling Anabasis, *Xenophon recalls the dramatic moment when, after months of horrendous hardships, the exhausted remnants of the Ten Thousand at last reached the coast of the familiar Black Sea, hopeful it was their route to freedom and home.*

"[We] reached the mountain in the fifth day [after a local guide had promised to show them the way to the sea]. . . . When the first men reached the summit and caught sight of the sea there was loud shouting. [I] and the rearguard, hearing this, thought that more enemies were attacking in front. . . . But when the shouts grew louder and nearer, as each group came up, [the good news] went pelting along to the shouting men in front, and the shouting was louder and louder as the crowds increased. [I] thought it must be something very important; [I] mounted my horse . . . and galloped to bring help. Soon [I] heard the soldiers shouting "The Sea! The Sea!" and passing the word along. Then the rearguard also broke into a run, and the horses and baggage animals galloped too. When they all reached the summit . . . they embraced each other, captains and officers and all, with tears running down their cheeks."

Catching sight of the Black Sea, soldiers of the Greek force later referred to as the Ten Thousand are overwhelmed with joy.

the central authority continued to weaken, rebellions cropped up in the east and also, once again, in Egypt; at this stage the Persian monarch and his military machine were not up to the task of crushing these uprisings. Artaxerxes failed to retake Egypt. And on a campaign against a rebellious tribe near the Caspian Sea, native guerrilla warfare was so effective against his army that he had to resort to bribing the rebel leaders into quitting the fight.

Thus, the Persian Empire, when inherited by Artaxerxes III, who became king at his father's death in 358, was more troubled and fragile than at any time in its history.[83] The new king managed to reconquer Egypt only with great difficulty, and large parts of the eastern half of the empire remained independent of his control during his reign. Before he could mount new offensives to recapture these lost lands, in 338 he was assassinated by one of his own advisers, Bagoas, who also killed all of the royal princes except the youngest. This unfortunate youth, named Arses, reigned as Bagoas's puppet for less than two years until meeting the same fate as his father and brothers. Bagoas next selected as king an obscure Achaemenid kinsman named Codomannus, who, after being crowned Darius III, had the good sense to kill the murderous kingmaker before he himself became the next royal victim.

Philip, Alexander, and the Anti-Persian Crusade

The chief distinction of Darius III's reign was that he was destined to be the last ruler of the Achaemenid dynasty. In a way he was a tragic character, for in contrast to many of his immediate predecessors, he appears to have been a mild-mannered and generous person who only wanted the best for his country. Had the circumstances of his reign been normal, he might have brought efficient and enlightened rule back to Persia.

However, circumstances at the time that Darius ascended the throne were far from normal. On the one hand, his military generals, satraps, and other officials had all they could do to keep the empire functioning and intact. On the other, a dangerous new situation had arisen in Greece. For years the Greek states had continued to battle and batter one another until they were nearly as militarily exhausted as Persia was. They had also failed to take seriously the increasing threat from the northern Greek kingdom of Macedonia, long viewed as a cultural and military backwash. But in 359 a tough, politically shrewd, and militarily brilliant individual, Philip II, assumed the throne and rapidly turned Macedonia into a world power. In 338, two years before Darius assumed his own throne, Philip decisively defeated a united Greek army led by Athens and Thebes at Chaeronea, west of Thebes, and became "captain-general" of a new, Macedonian-controlled Greece.

The threat that Philip posed to Persia became clear when, not long after his victory at Chaeronea, he began preparations for a large-scale invasion of Asia. Officially he claimed to be avenging Darius's and Xerxes' invasions of Greece a century and a half before, but his real motives were probably personal ambition and a staunch belief in the superiority of Greek culture. The Persians undoubtedly breathed a sigh of relief when Philip was assassinated in

One of the hundreds of modern depictions of the Greek general Alexander the Great, here seen mounted on his magnificent steed Bucephalas.

336. But relief soon turned to anxiety when his son, Alexander, stepped into his father's shoes.

As brilliant and ambitious as Philip, and ingrained with Aristotle's teachings that it was right and proper for Greeks to rule over so-called barbarians, Alexander zealously took up the anti-Persian crusade. In 334, at the age of only twenty-two, he led a crack combat force made up of 32,000 infantry and 5,000 cavalry across the Hellespont into Asia Minor. At the Granicus River, east of the Hellespont, he defeated a Persian army commanded by three local satraps, then marched on a winding path through their territories until he reached northwestern Syria. There, at Issus, Darius himself awaited him with a large army. Again Alexander won the day, although, due to impressive tactical plan-

ning by Darius, the victory was by no means overwhelming. Greek casualties numbered about 450 killed and 4,000 wounded, compared to some 15,000 Persians killed, wounded, or captured. When they overran the Persian camp, the Greeks also captured the Great King's wife, children, and mother, all of whom Alexander treated with kindness and respect.

Alexander and Darius then exchanged letters, the substance of which has survived in the Greek historian Arrian's account of the invasion. Darius told his adversary:

> Alexander has sent no representative to [my] court to confirm the former friendship and alliance between the two kingdoms; on the contrary, he has crossed into Asia with his armed forces and done much damage to the Persians. For this reason [I] took the field in defense of [my] country and of [my] ancestral throne. . . . Now Darius the King asks Alexander the King to restore from captivity his wife, his mother, and his children, and is willing to make friends with him and be his ally. For this cause [I] urge Alexander to send to [me] . . . representatives of his own in order that proper guarantees may be exchanged.

Alexander answered Darius:

> Your ancestors invaded . . . Greece and caused havoc in our country, though we had done nothing to provoke them. As supreme commander of all Greece I invaded Asia because I wished to punish Persia for this act. . . . First I defeated in battle your generals and satraps; now I have defeated yourself and the army you led. By God's help I am master of your country, and I have made myself responsible for the

The Struggle on the Riverbank

"There was a profound hush as both armies stood for a while motionless on the brink of the river, as if in awe of what was to come. Then Alexander . . . at the head of the right wing of the army, with trumpets blaring and the shout going up to the God of Battle, moved forward into the river. . . . The leading files [of his army] . . . were met as they gained the river bank by volleys of missiles from the Persians, who kept up a continuous fire into the river both from their commanding position on the high ground above, and also from the comparatively flat strip right down by the water's edge. A hand-to-hand struggle developed, the Greek mounted troops trying to force their way out of the water, the Persians doing their utmost to prevent them. Persian lances flew thick and fast, the long Greek spears thrust and stabbed. In the first onslaught Alexander's men, heavily outnumbered, suffered severely. . . . It was a cavalry battle with, as it were, infantry tactics: horse against horse, man against man, locked together, the Greeks did their utmost to thrust the enemy . . . back from the river bank . . . while the Persians fought to . . . hurl their opponents back into the water."

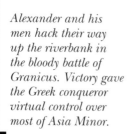

Alexander and his men hack their way up the riverbank in the bloody battle of Granicus. Victory gave the Greek conqueror virtual control over most of Asia Minor.

survivors of your army who fled to me for refuge: far from being detained by force, they are serving of their own free will under my command. Come to me, therefore, as you would come to the lord of the continent of Asia. . . . And in the future let any communication you wish to make with me be addressed to the King of all Asia. Do not write to me as an equal . . . or I shall take steps to deal with you as a criminal.[84]

Darius's Last, Gallant Gesture

As Darius had already learned the hard way, there was deadly substance behind Alexander's arrogant bravado. The Great King hurriedly began raising another army; but in the meantime he had to endure new humiliations heaped upon him by the Greek leader. Among them was Alexander's triumphant entry into Egypt in 332. There, after nearly two centuries of repeated strife with Persia, the natives joyfully welcomed the Greeks as liberators. The following year, with an expanded army of forty thousand infantry and seven thousand cavalry, Alexander marched northwest toward the Persian heartland.

On October 1, 331, at Gaugamela, a few miles southeast of the ruins of Assyrian Nineveh, Darius made his last stand at the head of a force of about one hundred thousand, including units of Saka and Bactrian cavalry, some two hundred war chariots, and fifteen battle elephants. The battle raged until Alexander charged with his veteran cavalry unit directly at the Great King's position. According to Plutarch, Darius's bodyguards

Alexander's troops congregate around the renowned Great Sphinx after their triumphant entry into Egypt.

were seized with panic at the terrible sight of Alexander bearing down upon them. . . . As for Darius, all the horrors of the battle were now before his eyes. The forces which had been stationed in the center for his protection had now been driven back upon him. . . . In this extremity the king abandoned his chariot and his armor, mounted a mare . . . and rode away.[85]

As the news of Darius's flight filtered through the ranks, most of his troops followed his lead.

After his great victory, Alexander pursued Darius for many miles before giving up the chase. The Greek king then moved unopposed into the Persian homeland of Fars, where, as thousands of horrified natives watched helplessly, he burned much of the magnificent capital of Persepolis. In June 330, Alexander struck out again after Darius, who was on the way to Bactria in the custody of Bessus, the Bactrian satrap, and other high Persian officials. Bessus had illegally declared himself the new Great King and planned, in the event that Alexander caught up with him, to exchange his royal prisoner for favorable terms. But when Bessus learned that the Greek leader was approaching, he and his supporters panicked, stabbed Darius with their javelins, and fled.

Perhaps less than an hour later, one of Alexander's men, Polystratus, thirsty after the long pursuit, stopped to drink from a stream. He noticed a driverless covered wagon nearby and then heard faint groans from within. On investigating, he found poor Darius, his body chained and blood soaked, accompanied only by his faithful dog. The king begged faintly for water and Polystratus gave him some. Then, taking the other man's hand, Darius whispered, "This is the final stroke of misfortune, that I should accept a service from you, and not be able to return it, but Alexander will reward you for your kindness, and the gods will repay him for his courtesy towards my mother and my wife and my children. And so through you, I give him my hand."[86] With these gallant and touching words, Darius quietly died.

When the news of the Great King's death reached Susa, Ecbatana, and what remained of Persepolis, people wailed and tore their clothes. They mourned partly for this gentle, well-meaning man who had perished before he could realize his bright potential; but they were also gripped by a deeper anguish and dread born of the realization that their ruler's death signaled a more profound passing. The Persians now faced the same terrible reality that their ancestors had long ago forced on the Medians, Babylonians, and others. The once grand Achaemenid empire was doomed to the fate that all human endeavors, no matter how mighty, inevitably share: to be swept by the relentless tides of history into oblivion's dark and eternal embrace.

Old Wounds Unhealed:
Iran Through the Ages

Over the centuries that followed the collapse of the Persian Empire, the lands formerly ruled by the Achaemenids were home to many diverse peoples, nations, and empires. The first of the empires, that of Persia's destroyer, Alexander, was both the largest and the shortest-lived. After capturing and punishing Bessus for murdering Darius, Alexander moved on through the eastern Persian satrapies, including Parthia and Bactria, and eventually reached India.[87] There, at the Hydapses River, he defeated a large Indian army; but he did not pursue the conquest of India because his men, exhausted from the long campaign, demanded that he turn back. Reluctantly he did so, and shortly after reaching Babylon in 323 B.C. he died unexpectedly (possibly of malaria) at the age of thirty-three. At that moment, his empire stretched from India in the east to Macedonia in the west.

But this vast realm barely outlived its creator. Not long after Alexander's passing, his leading generals fell into a power struggle over who should succeed him; appropriately, they became known as the *Diadochi,* or Successors. These ambitious men waged a series of devastating wars that lasted over forty years. Finally, by about 280, three large kingdoms emerged in what had been Alexander's empire; the biggest, founded by Seleucus, encompassed large parts of the former Persian heartland, along with sections of Palestine and Asia Minor.

Like its rival kingdoms, the Seleucid realm followed Alexander's lead and spread Greek language and culture throughout the eastern Mediterranean and Near East. Because native cultures often incorporated Greek ideas and customs, producing hybrid "Hellenistic," or "Greek-like," versions, scholars refer to the roughly three-century-long period following Alexander's conquests as the Hellenistic Age. Ironically, during these years the former Persians readily adopted many aspects of the Greek culture that their immediate ancestors had fought so hard to destroy. As Chester Starr points out:

> The Seleucid line [dynasty] particularly sought to build up a solid Greek framework in its far-flung domains and performed yeoman service in establishing Greek cities. . . . In Asia Minor some 80 colonies were founded by

rulers of various houses, and a dense network of Greek cities was built up in Syria. Both areas thenceforth had a Greek veneer [outer appearance] down to Arab days.[88]

Parthians, Sassanians, and Arabs

But while Greek culture exerted a strong influence in the Near East, the political and military systems of the Hellenistic rulers proved less influential and durable. Only a few decades after the creation of the Seleucid realm, its control over the old Persian heartland, including the lower Iranian plateau and eastern Mesopotamia, began to face serious challenges. In 238 nomadic Iranian tribesmen who had earlier migrated from central Asia seized most of the old Persian satrapy of Parthia. Their leader, Arsaces, founded the Parthian dynasty, the power and territories of which steadily grew at the expense of those of the Seleucid rulers.

By 141, the Seleucid Empire had been completely supplanted by the Parthian Empire. The Parthians thrived for more than three centuries, partly because they were the middlemen in the lucrative "silk route" over which luxury goods traveled from China in the east, to the by now Roman-controlled Mediterranean world in the west. Parthian rulers maintained good relations with Chinese leaders; but Parthian-Roman relations were strained, leading to periodic battles and wars between Parthia and Rome, particularly over control of the area of Armenia, which had been one of the Achaemenids' most important satrapies.

Eventually, Parthian power declined and in A.D. 224 the last Parthian king, Artabanus V, was overthrown by Ardashir, a popular local leader from the old Persian stronghold of Fars. Claiming descent from a noble named Sasan, Ardashir founded the Sassanian dynasty, which ruled Iran for more than four hundred years. According to John Curtis, the Sassanians

saw themselves as the successors to the Achaemenids, after the Hellenistic and Parthian interlude, and perceived it as their role to restore the greatness of Iran. Such ambitions inevitably brought the Sassanian monarchs into conflict with Rome and later Byzantium [located on the Bosporus] in the west, and war on that front was to become a constant refrain of Sassanian history. . . . In order to create a

An exquisite relief on a silver bowl shows a Sassanian monarch hunting lions. Lion hunting was a common artistic theme of Persia's Sassanian period.

state that could fulfill his grandiose schemes, Ardashir introduced strong central government, reformed the coinage, and made Zoroastrianism the state religion.[89]

Iran's Sassanian period came to a sudden and violent end between 637 and 651 when the forces of the last Sassanian king, Yazdigrid III, were defeated by an Arab army, part of a zealous Islamic crusade that swept through the Near East and northern Africa. The religious and cultural influence of Islam, introduced in this period, remains strong in Iran today.

As the centuries passed, other cultures and dynasties left their mark on the region. In the eleventh and twelfth centuries, the Seljuk Turks held sway, imparting a strong administrative and economic structure that largely endured to the opening of the twentieth century. In the sixteenth century, Shah Ismail established the Safavid dynasty in Iran. His contribution was the restoration, after many centuries, of Persia as a political entity (though this new Persia was a good deal smaller than the Achaemenid realm). In the centuries that followed, local native dynasties with little power and influence beyond the Iranian plateau came and went.

Iran in Modern Times

The modern state of Iran emerged after World War I when Reza Shah Pahlavi ascended the throne. He developed new industries and revised the legal system. His son, Muhammad Reza Shah Pahlavi, who became shah in 1941 at the age of twenty-two with the strong backing of Western leaders, later inaugurated an ambitious modernization program that became known as the White Revolution. Iran benefited from major land reform and rapid industrialization, largely funded by profits from the sale of the country's rich oil deposits. To help boost patriotism and pride in the past, the shah also revived interest in the original Achaemenid Persian rulers and their empire. In 1971 he spent over $300 million on a national celebration of the 2,500th anniversary of the Achaemenid monarchy;[90] and, firmly identifying himself as the modern successor of Cyrus the Great, he staged a solemn and elaborate ceremony at Cyrus's tomb.

However, many Iranians felt that the shah's ambitious programs had brought too much change too fast and had allowed Western influences to "corrupt" the country. In 1978 Pahlavi was forced to institute martial law to keep order and the following year he fled Iran. The opposition leader, Ayatollah Khomeini, a strict Islamic fundamentalist, then led an ultra-conservative revolution that made Iran an Islamic republic in which Western ideas and customs were discouraged. Though Khomeini died in 1989, his staunchly anti-Western adherents still maintain control of the country. Ironically, and perhaps tragically, nearly 2,500 years after Darius's and Xerxes' invasions of Greece initiated tensions between Europe and Asia, the old wounds have not fully healed and the gap in trust and understanding between East and West remains.

Notes

Introduction: The Villains of the Piece?

1. Isocrates, *Panegyricus*, in Paul J. Alexander, ed., *The Ancient World: To 300 A.D.* New York: Macmillan, 1963, p. 163.

2. Aristotle, *Politics*, in *The Philosophy of Aristotle*. Translated by A. E. Wardman and J. L. Creed. New York: New American Library, 1963, pp. 389–90.

3. A. T. Olmstead, *History of the Persian Empire*. Chicago: University of Chicago Press, 1948, p. viii.

4. Olmstead, *Persian Empire*, p. xi.

Chapter 1: The Ancient Near East: A Crossroads of Cultures

5. The literal meaning of Mesopotamia is "the land between the rivers," but historically the term has come to describe more generally all of the flatlands of the dual river system, a region inhabited by diverse nations and peoples over the millennia.

6. Chester G. Starr, *A History of the Ancient World*. New York: Oxford University Press, 1991, pp. 32–33.

7. "The Assyrians," in Sir John Hackett, ed., *Warfare in the Ancient World*. New York: Facts On File, 1989, pp. 36–37.

8. Olmstead, *Persian Empire*, p. 31.

9. Iranian horsemen, both Median and Persian, must have been widely feared and respected, for various Near Eastern peoples paid homage to them in coining words for the horse. Many Mesopotamian texts call the horse the "ass of the east" (Iran being east of Mesopotamia), and one ancient Hebrew name for the horse was *sus*, after Susa, long one of Persia's capitals.

10. *The Book of Nahum*/2:1–10, 3:1–3, in *The Holy Bible*. Revised Standard Version. New York: Thomas Nelson & Sons, 1962, pp. 729–30. Nahum was a Hebrew prophet who lived in the late seventh century B.C., the era in which the Medes, then overlords of the Persians, were rising to power. His Old Testament narrative is valuable for its moving description of the sacking of the Assyrian capital of Nineveh by the Medes and Babylonians, which he probably heard about from eyewitnesses.

11. The conquerors so efficiently erased vestiges of native Assyrian culture and monuments that when, only slightly more than two centuries later, the Greek soldier-historian Xenophon passed by the crumbling ruins of Nineveh, his Persian guides could not confirm who had originally built the city.

12. Alessandro Bausani, *The Persians: From the Earliest Days to the Twentieth Century*. Translated by J. B. Donne. London: Elek Books, 1971, p. 15.

13. Herodotus, *The Histories*. Translated by Aubrey de Sélincourt. New York: Penguin Books, 1972, p. 70.

Chapter 2: A Man of Vision and Talent: Cyrus the Great Builds an Empire

14. Bausani, *The Persians*, pp. 15–16.

15. Herodotus, *The Histories*, p. 95.

16. Nick Sekunda, "The Persians," in Hackett, *Warfare in the Ancient World*, pp. 83–84.

17. Xenophon, *Cyropaedia*, vol. 2. Translated by Walter Miller. New York: Macmillan, 1914, pp. 135–37.

18. Herodotus, *The Histories*, pp. 72–73.

19. Herodotus, *The Histories*, pp. 78–79.

20. The Spartans' refusal to send troops was not motivated by fear, for they feared no one. But they were traditionally reclusive, going to

war only when they perceived threats to their national interests. They perceived the Ionian cities as far away and not worth the loss of Spartan troops.

21. Quoted in Herodotus, *The Histories*, p. 103. Cyrus's mention of "meeting places" was a disdainful reference to Greek *agorae*, or marketplaces. The early Persians had no such open markets and considered them undignified.

22. Olmstead, *Persian Empire*, p. 44.

23. The famous dramatic accounts of the fall of Babylon given by Herodotus (*The Histories*) and Xenophon (*Cyropaedia*), in which Cyrus lays siege to the city and later diverts the waters of the Euphrates so that his men can attack from the riverbed, are now known to be incorrect. In reality, Cyrus earlier drained a section of the Tigris in order to take the city of Opis. Apparently, the Greek historians, writing a century or more later, mistakenly transferred the operation to Babylon.

24. Quoted in Olmstead, *Persian Empire*, p. 51.

25. Bausani, *The Persians*, p. 18.

26. Xenophon, *Cyropaedia*, vol. 1, p. 11.

Chapter 3: Cambyses and Darius: The Empire Expands

27. Herodotus, *The Histories*, p. 243.

28. It is uncertain whether Cambyses actually used the ships during the desert crossing. According to Herodotus, the king made a deal with some local Arab sheiks, who supplied his army with trains of camels carrying containers of water. In any case, Cambyses did build a fleet at this time.

29. Herodotus, *The Histories*, p. 215.

30. Quoted in Andrew R. Burn, *Persia and the Greeks: The Defense of the West, c. 546–478 B.C.* London: Edward Arnold, 1962, p. 90.

31. Quoted in Burn, *Persia and the Greeks*, p. 93.

32. Quoted in Burn, *Persia and the Greeks*, p. 92.

33. Percy Sykes, *A History of Persia*. 2 vols. 1915. Reprint, London: Macmillan, 1958, pp. 160–61.

34. Bausani, *The Persians*, pp. 21–22.

35. The exception was the Persian homeland, Fars (Persis), which, because it was not considered a satrapy, was not obliged to pay taxes.

36. Herodotus, *The Histories*, pp. 359–60.

Chapter 4: Of Sovereigns, Serfs, and Slaves: Life in the Persian Heartland

37. Herodotus, *The Histories*, p. 97.

38. Bausani, *The Persians*, p. 16.

39. Xenophon, *Cyropaedia*, vol. 2, pp. 355–57.

40. Olmstead, *Persian Empire*, p. 77.

41. Herodotus, *The Histories*, p. 97.

42. Herodotus, *The Histories*, p. 98.

43. Xenophon, *Cyropaedia*, vol. 2, pp. 193–95.

44. Quoted in Bausani, *The Persians*, p. 27.

45. Herodotus, *The Histories*, p. 98.

46. Herodotus, *The Histories*, pp. 96–97.

47. Olmstead, *Persian Empire*, p. 117.

48. This teaching does not seem to square with Darius's and his son Xerxes' blatant conquests of neighboring lands, which suggests that they interpreted "neighbors" more narrowly to mean equals, that is, other upper-class Persians. From this perspective, since foreigners were inferior to Persians, other nations were not necessarily worthy of neighborly treatment.

49. According to Christian tradition, three Magi traveled from "the east" into Palestine in the late first century B.C., bearing gifts for the infant Jesus. Many later Christian artistic depictions, for instance some found in the Roman catacombs (dating from the second

century A.D.), show these Magi wearing traditional Persian robes.

Chapter 5: A Stepping-Stone to Europe: Darius Versus the Greeks

50. Archaeologists have found such cups, neatly trimmed in gold and bronze, in Scythian tombs.

51. Herodotus, *The Histories*, p. 310.

52. Herodotus, *The Histories*, pp. 312–13.

53. John Warry, *Warfare in the Classical World*. Norman: University of Oklahoma Press, 1995, p. 25.

54. Herodotus, *The Histories*, p. 379.

55. Herodotus, *The Histories*, p. 382.

56. Herodotus tells how all but eleven of the sixty vessels in the contingent from Samos fled the battle. The officers of these eleven ships "stayed and fought contrary to orders from their superiors," and soon most if not all of them, along with their crews, perished in the fighting. Years later, the Samian government erected a monument to honor their bravery.

57. Herodotus, *The Histories*, pp. 394–95.

58. Herodotus, *The Histories*, p. 403.

59. Herodotus, *The Histories*, p. 424.

60. These captives were taken back to Persia and settled in a remote region about thirty miles from Susa. More than five hundred years later, the first-century A.D. Greek sage and adventurer Apollonius of Tyana visited the area and there found their descendants, still speaking their ancestral tongue and holding dear the memory of their former homeland.

61. Herodotus, *The Histories*, p. 429.

Chapter 6: An Enormous Potential Unfulfilled: Xerxes Versus the Greeks

62. Herodotus, *The Histories*, p. 441.

63. Quoted in Burn, *Persia and the Greeks*, p. 278.

64. Quoted in Herodotus, *The Histories*, p. 444.

65. Herodotus, *The Histories*, pp. 457–58.

66. Herodotus, *The Histories*, p. 454.

67. Herodotus, *The Histories*, p. 457.

68. Herodotus, *The Histories*, p. 459.

69. These estimates are by modern historians and military experts. Herodotus's figures, including 1,750,000 infantry, 100,000 mounted troops, 510,000 sailors, and over 2 million camp personnel, are hugely exaggerated, for so gigantic a host could not have sustained itself on the march.

70. Herodotus, *The Histories*, p. 464.

71. Herodotus, *The Histories*, p. 504.

72. Diodorus Siculus, *Library of History*, vol. 4. Translated by Charles L. Sherman and C. Bradford Welles. Cambridge, MA: Harvard University Press, 1963, pp. 139–41.

73. Herodotus, *The Histories*, p. 541.

74. Quoted in Aeschylus, *The Persians*, in *Aeschylus: Prometheus Bound, The Suppliants, Seven Against Thebes, The Persians*. Translated by Philip Vellacott. Baltimore: Penguin Books, 1961, p. 134.

75. Quoted in Herodotus, *The Histories*, p. 557.

76. The League, also referred to as the Confederacy of Delos, was so named because the initial congress of states took place on the tiny sacred island of Delos, strategically located in the center of the Aegean.

Chapter 7: The Pale Shadow of a Great Empire: Persia's Decline and Fall

77. Diodorus, *Library of History*, p. 311.

78. Megabyzus rebelled to protest the brutal treatment of the leading prisoners he had taken during the Egyptian campaign. He had promised on his honor to spare the lives of Inaros and the Greek generals; however, pressed incessantly by the mean-spirited

Amestris, the king negated Megabyzus's agreement, ordering the impalement of Inaros and beheading of the Greeks.

79. Plutarch, *Artaxerxes*, in *Lives of the Noble Grecians and Romans*, published complete as *Plutarch's Lives*. Translated by John Dryden. New York: Random House, 1932, p. 1,252.

80. Xenophon, *Anabasis*, published as *The March Up Country*. Translated by W. H. D. Rouse. New York: New American Library, 1959, p. 38.

81. Xenophon, *Anabasis*, p. 66.

82. Agesilaus is famous for joking that Artaxerxes had driven him out of Asia with "ten thousand archers." As Plutarch points out, this was a reference to the fact that "the gold coins of Persia at this time were stamped with the figure of an archer" (see Plutarch, *Agesilaus*, in *Lives of the Noble Grecians and Romans*, excerpted in *Plutarch: The Age of Alexander*. Translated by Ian Scott-Kilvert. New York: Penguin Books, 1973, p. 40).

83. The new king was so anxious about the throne's precarious position that once in power he murdered all of his brothers and sisters so as to forestall any potential rebellions by ambitious kinfolk.

84. Arrian, *Anabasis Alexandri*, published as *The Campaigns of Alexander*. Translated by Aubrey de Sélincourt. New York: Penguin Books, 1971, pp. 126–28.

85. Plutarch, *Alexander*, in *Plutarch: The Age of Alexander*, p. 291.

86. Quoted in Plutarch, *Alexander*, p. 300.

Epilogue: Old Wounds Unhealed: Iran Through the Ages

87. For Alexander's harsh treatment of Bessus, see Plutarch, *Alexander*, pp. 300–301, and Arrian, *Anabasis*, p. 212.

88. Starr, *Ancient World*, p. 407.

89. Curtis, *Ancient Persia*, p. 61.

90. Interestingly, counting backward 2,500 years from 1971 one arrives at the date of 529 B.C. This year had no known significance as a Persian founding date. The shah's reasons for choosing these numbers are unclear.

For Further Reading

Isaac Asimov, *The Greeks: A Great Adventure.* Boston: Houghton Mifflin, 1965. An excellent, entertaining overview of Greek history and culture, including relations and wars with Persia.

Peter Connolly, *The Greek Armies.* Morristown, NJ: Silver Burdett, 1979. A fine, detailed study of Greek armor, weapons, and battle tactics, including those used against the Persians. Filled with colorful, accurate illustrations by Connolly, the world's leading artistic interpreter of the ancient world. Highly recommended.

Michael W. Davison, ed., *Everyday Life Through the Ages.* London: Reader's Digest Association, 1992. This large, beautifully illustrated volume, which examines the way people lived in various cultures throughout history, has a section on ancient Persia, as well as sections on ancient Assyria, Babylonia, and Greece.

Harold Lamb, *Cyrus the Great.* Garden City, NY: Doubleday, 1960. This fascinating modern telling of the life and times of Cyrus, founder of the Persian Empire, is written in a straightforward style and should be accessible to both high-schoolers and ambitious junior high-schoolers.

Hazel M. Martell, *The Ancient World: From the Ice Age to the Fall of Rome.* New York: Kingfisher, 1995. A very handsomely mounted book that briefly examines the various important ancient civilizations, including many of those mentioned in this volume about ancient Persia.

Don Nardo, *Ancient Greece.* San Diego: Lucent Books, 1994; *The Battle of Marathon.* San Diego: Lucent Books, 1996; *The Age of Pericles.* San Diego: Lucent Books, 1996; and *Philip and Alexander: The Unification of Greece.* New York: Franklin Watts, forthcoming in 1998. These volumes provide much useful background information about Greek-Persian relations, from the first contact between the two peoples in the sixth century B.C. to the destruction of the Persian Empire by Alexander the Great in the 320s B.C., along with synopses of the major battles and sketches of the important political and military figures.

Works Consulted

Ancient Sources

Aeschylus, *The Persians*, in *Aeschylus: Prometheus Bound, The Suppliants, Seven Against Thebes, The Persians*. Translated by Philip Vellacott. Baltimore: Penguin Books, 1961. Born about 524 B.C., the Athenian playwright Aeschylus has long been acknowledged as the world's first great dramatist. Scholars believe that he wrote at least eighty plays; of the seven that have survived, *The Persians*, about the Greek victory over the Persian fleet at Salamis in 480 B.C., is the only one that deals with nonmythological events. More importantly, the play describes events Aeschylus himself took part in, for he is thought to have fought at Salamis (as well as at Marathon a decade earlier). Although the style of the play is poetic and the author employs a certain amount of dramatic license, the description of the battle itself has the ring of an eyewitness account and historians have more or less accepted its authenticity.

Aristotle, *Politics*, in *The Philosophy of Aristotle*. Translated by A. E. Wardman and J. L. Creed. New York: New American Library, 1963. Aristotle, the fourth-century B.C. Greek philosopher, scholar, and teacher of Alexander the Great, wrote a large number of works on diverse subjects, some of which survived to profoundly influence the thinking of scholars in Europe's Middle Ages and Renaissance. Some of Aristotle's ideas also had indirect yet far-reaching influence in his own time. His *Politics*, an examination of the purpose of the state and of the place of human beings within it, expounds the theories he preached to Alexander, namely that some persons are born "natural slaves," among these all barbarians (or non-Greeks). Indoctrinated with Aristotle's view that it was right and fitting for Greeks to rule over barbarians, Alexander proceeded to invade Asia and subjugate the Persians.

Arrian, *Anabasis Alexandri*, published as *The Campaigns of Alexander*. Translated by Aubrey de Sélincourt. New York: Penguin Books, 1971. Arrian was a Greek, born about A.D. 90 in the Roman province of Bithynia in Asia Minor. Unfortunately, most of his other important works, including *Indike*, about Greek and Roman contacts with distant India, *Events After Alexander* (in ten books), and the *History of Bithynia*, are either lost or survive only in a few fragments. Because his *Anabasis* (not to be confused with Xenophon's work of the same name; see below) was based largely on now lost histories written by Alexander's general, Ptolemy, and by Aristobulus, an engineer under Alexander, both of whom witnessed Alexander's campaigns firsthand, historians consider much of Arrian's account to be reasonably accurate.

Diodorus Siculus, *Library of History*, vol. 4. Translated by Charles L. Sherman and C. Bradford Welles. Cambridge, MA:

Harvard University Press, 1963. Diodorus, a Sicilian Greek of the first century B.C. (when Sicily was under Roman rule), traveled extensively around the Mediterranean world and collected many ancient documents and histories that are now lost. His massive *Library of History* (also variously referred to as his *World History* or *Universal History*) was originally composed of forty books, about fifteen of which survive complete or almost so. About ten of these cover inclusively the years 480 to 302 B.C., which includes most of the Greek and Persian Wars, as well as the decline and fall of the Persian Empire. As a writer, Diodorus was largely unoriginal and uninspired, and he tended to repeat and even contradict himself; also, he sometimes failed to credit his sources. Nevertheless, his history is important because it preserves material from the lost histories he used as sources, works that covered time periods and events that would otherwise remain undocumented.

Herodotus, *The Histories*. Translated by Aubrey de Sélincourt. New York: Penguin Books, 1972. Herodotus was born about 480 B.C. in Asia Minor. In pursuit of information for his historical volume, the first known major European prose writing, he traveled extensively through the eastern Mediterranean, spending considerable time in Athens and finally dying in Italy in about 425. His *Histories* purports to be an account of the Greek and Persian Wars from the 490s to the 470s (which he viewed as the most momentous event in world history up to that time); but it is in fact much broader in scope, covering the backgrounds, religions, customs, cultural traits, and legends of dozens of peoples, including to a great extent the Persians, a veritable treasure house of detailed information he collected in his travels. Not all of what he recorded was accurate, for he often simply repeated what he heard; however, Herodotus created a huge and at the same time intricate portrait of the ancient world of his own era and the centuries immediately preceding it. Fortunately for later generations, he was an endlessly curious individual who wrote in a clear, graceful, storybook-like style that makes his masterwork highly entertaining reading. The nickname accorded him in later centuries, the "father of history," is in many ways well deserved.

Isocrates, *Panegyricus*, in Paul J. Alexander, ed., *The Ancient World: To 300 A.D.* New York: Macmillan, 1963. Born about 436 B.C., Isocrates was the most famous and influential of a group of Athenian orators who, in the first half of the fourth century B.C., called for the always squabbling Greek city-states to unite against the "barbarians," specifically the Persians. Whereas his *Panegyricus*, published in 380 B.C., was a general call to arms, his *Address to Philip*, issued in the 340s, was aimed directly at Macedonia's King Philip II, who at the time was on the verge of forcing the Greek states to unify under him. Because of Philip's untimely death a decade later, the task of invading Persia fell to his son, Alexander, who fulfilled old Isocrates' dreams by quickly toppling the more than two-century-old Achaemenid realm.

Isocrates' writings are characterized by blunt assertions of Greek ethnic and cultural superiority and blatant advocacy of violence, yet the merit of their underlying theme, that the key to Greece's survival lay in unity, became clear later when the still disunited Greek states fell to Rome.

Plutarch, *Artaxerxes*, in *Lives of the Noble Grecians and Romans*, excerpted in *Plutarch: The Age of Alexander*. Translated by Ian Scott-Kilvert. New York: Penguin Books, 1973; and published complete as *Plutarch's Lives*. Translated by John Dryden. New York: Random House, 1932. Plutarch was born about A.D. 46 at Chaeronea in eastern Greece. He was for a time a resident of Rome and greatly admired Roman civilization's accomplishments and heroes. These historical figures, along with many from his own Greek heritage, became the subjects of his massive collection of biographies (mostly written between 105 and 115), for which he is justly famous. Despite his tendency to moralize, Plutarch was a skilled writer and his works are colorful, detailed, and often dramatic. For the purposes of this volume, the most important of his biographies are those of Artaxerxes II, the Persian monarch who ruled from 404 to 359 B.C. and figured prominently in the events that led to the March of the Ten Thousand, in which the Greek historian Xenophon took part; and Alexander the Great, who conquered the Achaemenid Persians in the late fourth century B.C.; reference is also made to the biographies of Themistocles, Cimon, Aristides, and Agesilaus.

Xenophon, *Anabasis*, published as *The March Up Country*. Translated by W. H. D. Rouse. New York: New American Library, 1959; *Hellenica*, published as *A History of My Times*. Translated by Rex Warner. New York: Penguin Books, 1979; and *Cyropaedia*. 2 vols. Translated by Walter Miller. New York: Macmillan, 1914. Xenophon (pronounced ZEN-uh-phon), who was born in Athens about 428 B.C., led an unusually eventful and colorful life. As a young man he fought in the disastrous Peloponnesian War, which engulfed the Greek city-states, and he also became a friend and admirer of the famous philosopher Socrates. Later he fought as a mercenary in Asia, which led to his involvement in the heroic "March of the Ten Thousand." His account of this episode, the *Anabasis*, remains one of the most gripping adventure tales ever written and is an important source of information about Persia during that era. His *Cyropaedia*, or *Education of Cyrus*, also contains important information about Persian history and military organization. Unfortunately, while Xenophon could describe with considerable flair events he had personally taken part in, he was not a skilled historian. In his *Hellenica*, for instance, he not only regularly moralized about various people and policies, but also frequently glossed over or even entirely left out important historical figures and episodes. As one modern scholar puts it, "Overall his method was to write up what he already knew about, not to find out what he did not know." Similarly, sections of the *Cyropaedia* sacrifice historical accuracy for the sake of

Xenophon's attempt to construct a portrait of an ideal monarch, making the work more a historical novel than a true history (for example, Xenophon's Cyrus dies quietly in bed, whereas the real Cyrus died on the battlefield). Nevertheless, this and his other works are still valuable, partly because they contain often vivid and probably largely accurate descriptions of a number of the important events of his own time and of the century or so directly preceding it.

Modern Sources

Alessandro Bausani, *The Persians: From the Earliest Days to the Twentieth Century.* Translated by J. B. Donne. London: Elek Books, 1971. This volume is valuable mainly for its overview of Persia after its fall to Alexander the Great, including the Seleucid, Parthian, Sassanid, Arab, Seljuk, Mongol, and later modern periods.

Andrew R. Burn, *Persia and the Greeks: The Defense of the West, c. 546–478 B.C.* London: Edward Arnold, 1962. This masterful, scholarly work covers the rise of Persia under Cyrus the Great in the sixth century B.C., his conquest of the Greek Ionian cities, the Ionian revolt and its subsequent failure, and the Persian invasions of Greece under Darius's general Datis and later Darius's son Xerxes. Well written and carefully documented.

John Curtis, *Ancient Persia.* Cambridge, MA: Harvard University Press, 1990. A short but informative volume summarizing Persian history, ethnicity, art, and architecture.

Peter Green, *Alexander of Macedon, 356–323 B.C.: A Historical Biography.* Berkeley and Los Angeles: University of California Press, 1991. One of the best modern studies of Alexander, this detailed, well-researched volume by a widely respected historian contains much valuable information about the Persian Empire during its decline in the fourth century B.C.

———, *The Greco-Persian Wars.* Berkeley and Los Angeles: University of California Press, 1996. Another fine volume by Green, this is a detailed, heavily documented, up-to-date overview of relations between the Persians and Greeks, including excellent descriptions of the various military campaigns and engagements.

Sir John Hackett, ed., *Warfare in the Ancient World.* New York: Facts On File, 1989. This extremely informative and handsome volume is a collection of long, detailed essays by world-class historians, each of whom tackles the military development and methods of a single ancient people or empire. The beautiful and accurate illustrations are by the famous scholar-artist Peter Connolly (see For Further Reading). For this volume on the Persian Empire, I have consulted "The Assyrians" by D. J. Wiseman, which examines the Mesopotamian military machine that directly preceded and significantly influenced that of Persia; "The Persians" by Nick Sekunda; "Hoplite Warfare" by John Lazenby, a masterful sketch of the Greek armor, weapons, and tactics that repeatedly proved superior to those of the Persians; and "Alexander the Great" by Albert Divine, a fine synopsis of Alexander's battles against the Persians.

A. T. Olmstead, *History of the Persian Empire*. Chicago: University of Chicago Press, 1948. A huge scholarly work that covers, often in intricate detail, all aspects of ancient Persian history, ethnicity, social customs, government, military methods, art, architecture, and religion.

Percy Sykes, *A History of Persia*. 2 vols. 1915. Reprint, London: Macmillan, 1958. This massive work is now out of date in some respects, as many archaeological discoveries made since it was published are not taken into account; however, much basic information is still useful and many of Sykes's insights are interesting (if decidedly biased in favor of the Greeks and "higher" Western ideals). Of interest only to scholars.

John Warry, *Warfare in the Classical World*. Norman: University of Oklahoma Press, 1995. A beautifully mounted book filled with accurate and useful paintings, drawings, maps, and diagrams. The text is also first-rate, providing much detailed information about the weapons, clothing, strategies, battle tactics, and military leaders of the Greeks, Romans, and the peoples they fought, including the Persians.

Additional Works Consulted

C. W. Ceram, *Gods, Graves, and Scholars.* New York: Random House, 1979.

Peter A. Clayton and Martin J. Price, *The Seven Wonders of the Ancient World.* New York: Barnes and Noble Books, 1993.

J. M. Cook, *The Persian Empire.* London: Dent, 1983.

Ilya Gershevitch, ed., *The Cambridge History of Iran*, Vol. 2; *The Median and Achaemenian Periods.* Cambridge, England: Cambridge University Press, 1985.

Michael Grant, *From Alexander to Cleopatra: The Hellenistic World.* New York: Charles Scribner's Sons, 1982.

———, *The Classical Greeks.* New York: Scribner's, 1989.

———, *The Rise of the Greeks.* New York: Macmillan, 1987.

Victor David Hanson, *The Western Way to War: Infantry Battle in Classical Greece.* New York: Oxford University Press, 1989.

John Lazenby, *The Defense of Greece.* Bloomington, IL: David Brown, 1993.

Peter Levi, *Atlas of the Greek World.* New York: Facts On File, 1984.

Rustom Masani, *Zoroastrianism: Religion of the Good Life.* New York: Macmillan, 1968.

A. J. Podlecki, *The Life of Themistocles.* Montreal: McGill-Queen's University Press, 1975.

Aubrey de Sélincourt, *The World of Herodotus.* San Francisco: North Point Press, 1982.

Chester G. Starr, *A History of the Ancient World.* New York: Oxford University Press, 1991.

Index

Picture Credits

About the Author

Classical historian and award-winning writer Don Nardo has published over eighty books. His studies related to this volume on ancient Persia include *The Battle of Marathon, The Age of Pericles, Greek and Roman Theater, Greek and Roman Mythology,* and *Philip and Alexander: The Unification of Greece.* In addition, he has written extensively about ancient Rome in such works as *The Roman Republic, The Punic Wars, The Age of Augustus,* and his biography of Julius Caesar. Mr. Nardo also writes screenplays and teleplays and composes music. He lives with his wife, Christine, and his dog, Bud, on Cape Cod, Massachusetts.